CRIMINAL JUSTICE
IN ILLINOIS TODAY

ELLEN G. COHN

CLYDE CRONKHITE

WESTERN ILLINOIS UNIVERSITY

Prentice Hall

Upper Saddle River, New Jersey 07458

Publisher: Jeff Johnston
Director of Production and Manufacturing: Bruce Johnson
Acquisitions Editor: Kim Davies
Editorial Assistant: Sarah Holle
Marketing Manager: Chris Ruel
Managing Editor: Mary Carnis
Manufacturing Manager: Ed O'Dougherty
Production Editor: Brian Hyland
Art Director: Marianne Frasco
Cover Design Coordinator: Miguel Ortiz
Cover Design: Denise Brown
Printing and Binding: Victor Graphics
Cover Printer: Victor Graphics

Prentice-Hall International (UK) Limited, *London*
Prentice-Hall of Australia Pty. Limited, *Sydney*
Prentice-Hall Canada Inc., *Toronto*
Prentice-Hall Hispanoamericana, S.A., *Mexico*
Prentice-Hall of India Private Limited, *New Delhi*
Prentice-Hall of Japan, Inc., *Tokyo*
Prentice-Hall Singapore Pte. Ltd.
Editora Prentice-Hall do Brasil, Ltda., *Rio de Janeiro*

Copyright © 2001 by Prentice-Hall, Inc., Upper Saddle River, New Jersey 07458. All rights reserved. Printed in the United States of America. This publication is protected by Copyright and permission should be obtained from the publisher prior to any prohibited reproduction, storage in a retrieval system, or transmission in any form or by any means, electronic, mechanical, photocopying, recording, or likewise. For Information regarding permission(s), write to: Rights and Permissions Department.

10 9 8 7 6 5 4 3 2 1
ISBN 0-13-089850-3

TABLE OF CONTENTS

Preface v

Chapter 1   **The State of Illinois** 1
                     Introduction 1
                     The History of Illinois 1
                     Illinois Today 6

Chapter 2   **Introduction to Illinois Criminal Law** 9
                     The Structure of the Government 9
                     The Criminal Law in Illinois 12
                     The Definition and Classification of Crime 13
                     Defenses To a Criminal Charge 16

Chapter 3   **Index Crimes** 23
                     Introduction 23
                     Criminal Homicide 23
                     Forcible Rape/Criminal Sexual Assault 29
                     Robbery 31
                     Assault and Battery 34
                     Burglary 35
                     Larceny-Theft 36
                     Motor Vehicle Theft 39
                     Arson 39
                     Hate Crimes 40

Chapter 4   **The Police in Illinois** 43
                     Introduction 43
                     Local Policing 43
                     County Policing 47
                     State Policing 51
                     Police Training 55

Chapter 5   **The Court System in Illinois** 59
                     The History of the Illinois Court System 59
                     United States Federal Courts 61
                     The Illinois Supreme Court 62
                     Illinois Appellate Courts 63
                     Illinois Circuit Courts 64
                     Court Administration 64
                     Illinois Criminal Court Procedures 66

Chapter 6	**Sentencing in Illinois**	77
	Introduction	77
	Types of Sentences	77
	When Sentencing Occurs	78
	Determinate and Indeterminate Sentencing	80
	Concurrent Versus Consecutive Sentences	80
	Sentences of Incarceration	81
	Aggravating and Mitigating Circumstances	82
	Restitution and Fines	85
	Other Possible Sentences	86
	Victim Rights and Services	87
Chapter 7	**Capital Punishment in Illinois**	91
	Capital Punishment in Illinois Today	91
	Sentencing in Capital Crimes	91
	The Moratorium on Executions in Illinois	96
Chapter 8	**Corrections in Illinois**	97
	The Illinois Department of Corrections	97
	Prisons in Illinois	99
	Prison Labor	102
	Jails in Illinois	103
	Community Supervision Programs in Illinois	105
	Becoming a Correctional Officer	110
Chapter 9	**The Juvenile Justice System in Illinois**	111
	Introduction	111
	The Problem of Juvenile Crime in Illinois	112
	The Department of Corrections - Juvenile Justice Division	112
	Juvenile Field Services	114
	What Happens to a Juvenile Who is Arrested in Illinois?	114
	Teen Courts	118
Chapter 10	**Drugs and Crime in Illinois**	121
	Introduction	121
	The Office of Alcoholism and Substance Abuse	121
	Treatment Alternatives for Safe Communities	123
	Drug Courts in Illinois	125
Appendix	**Web Sites of Interest**	129

PREFACE

This supplementary text is designed to accompany Frank Schmalleger's *Criminal Justice Today, 6th edition*, published by Prentice Hall. It provides you with specific information on the Illinois criminal law and the Illinois criminal justice system. Throughout this supplement, you will find parenthetical references to page numbers in Schmalleger. The reference (see Schmalleger, p.25) means that the information given in the supplement relates to something discussed on page 25 of *Criminal Justice Today*.

Throughout the text, you will find quotations which have been taken verbatim from legal documents, such as the Illinois Compiled Statutes (ILCS) and the Illinois Constitution. Any misspellings or other irregularities are reproduced exactly as they appear in the original documents.

I hope that you enjoy this supplement and find it both interesting and informative. If you have any questions, comments, or suggestions, please feel free to contact me via email.

Ellen G. Cohn, Ph.D.
cohne@fiu.edu

CHAPTER 1

THE STATE OF ILLINOIS

INTRODUCTION

Illinois is located in the north central portion of the United States and has the largest population of any other Midwestern state. The largest city in the state is Chicago; approximately half the state's residents live in and around Chicago. The capital of the state is Springfield, which is located in the center of the state. The state bird is the cardinal, the state flower is the native or purple violet, the state tree is the white oak, and the state animal is the white-tailed deer. Illinois' nickname is the "Prairie State." The official state slogan is "The Land of Lincoln."

THE HISTORY OF ILLINOIS

Indian Occupation of Illinois

The area now known as Illinois was originally occupied by a variety of Native American tribes, including the Cahokia, Kaskaskia, Michigamea, Moingwena, Peoria, and Tamaroa peoples. These tribes, which belonged to the Algonquian family, were collectively known as the Illinois Confederacy. They controlled a large area, which included what is now Illinois, southern Wisconsin, and parts of Missouri and Iowa, until the late 1600s, when the Iroquois began to move westward and attacked the Illinois Indians. By 1800, only a few Illinois Indians remained, most of whom settled in Oklahoma.

French and British Control of Illinois

The first Europeans known to have reached Illinois were the French explorers, Father Jacques Marquette, a Roman Catholic missionary, and Louis Jolliet, a fur trader, in 1673. In 1675, Marquette returned to the area and founded a mission among the Kaskaskia Indians, near what is now Utica. In 1680, French traders built Fort Crevecoeur on the Illinois River, near what is today Peoria. Two years later, they built Fort St. Louis further up the river.

The first permanent settlement in the Illinois region was the town of Cahokia, which was founded in 1699 as a mission by French priests of the Quebec Seminary of Foreign Missions. In 1703 a group of Jesuit priests founded Kaskaskia on the Mississippi River. These two towns became the centers of French life in the area. In 1717, Illinois became part of Louisiana, a French colony.

That same year, John Law, a Scottish banker living in Paris developed the Mississippi Scheme which formed the Mississippi Company, an organization designed to colonize and develop the Mississippi River Valley, which lay in the Louisiana Territory. The company had exclusive trade rights in the territory for 25 years and controlled large land grants around the Mississippi River. The scheme was extremely popular and many French citizens bought shares in the company. Speculation significantly inflated the price of the shares. However, when shareholders discovered that the Mississippi Company did not actively develop business enterprises in America, they began to sell their shares at a significant loss. This resulted in a financial panic, known as the "bursting of the Mississippi Bubble," in 1720. Most investors suffered heavy losses from the scheme, but it did help to advertise Louisiana and did bring many colonists to Illinois.

In 1720 the French built a new fort, Fort de Chartres, on the east bank of the Mississippi River, about 20 miles northwest of Kaskaskia, to protect their settlements and investments in the Illinois region. The fort became the seat of France's military and civil government in the region. The fort was rebuilt in the 1750s.

Between 1689 and 1763, the French and the British, with various colonial and Indian allies, fought a series of four wars in North America for control and domination of the continent. In the United States today, these wars are collectively known as the French and Indian Wars. At this time, England's colonies were located along the Atlantic coast while the French settlements were primarily found further north, along the shores of the Great Lakes and the St. Lawrence River, as well as in the Mississippi River Valley. Both the French and the English traded with the Indians for furs. While England laid claim to all the territory inland of its own colonies, the French also claimed much of this land. The two countries each attempted to control the fur trade as well as the fishing grounds off the coast of Newfoundland. Both also claimed the land between the Appalachian Mountains and the Mississippi River.

The fourth of these wars, which ran from 1754 to 1763, was known in Europe and Canada as the Seven Years' War; in the United States it is often referred to as the French and Indian War. During this war, the French allied themselves with Pontiac, a chief of the Ottawa tribe who led his tribe in fighting with the French against the British. In 1763, the British defeated the French and the war ended with the signing of the Treaty of Paris. As a result of this treaty, Britain gained almost all of France's territorial possessions, including the Illinois region. However, Britain managed to antagonize the French settlers in Illinois who did not wish to live under British rule. As a result, many of them moved to St. Louis or New Orleans.

Shortly after the signing of the Treaty of Paris, Chief Pontiac led a confederacy of Native Americans in an uprising against the British, in an attempt to re-establish their autonomy in the area. The British had fourteen garrisons located between the Pennsylvania frontier and Lake Superior. The Indians captured all but four of these. Pontiac led the assault against the outpost at Detroit and failed to capture the garrison. He then began a five-month siege against the outpost, which ended when British reinforcements reached Detroit and Pontiac learned of a peace treaty between France and Britain which destroyed his hopes of French aid. In August, 1765, Pontiac entered into a formal peace treaty with the British.

In 1774, the passage of the Quebec Act by Parliament included an act which designated the land north of the Ohio River (including Illinois) to be part of Quebec Province. American colonists considered this to be one of the Intolerable Acts which punished the colonies for hostilities such as the Boston Tea Party. The anger generated by the Intolerable Acts contributed to the outbreak of the American Revolution.

Illinois as an American Territory

In 1778, George Rogers Clark of Virginia, with a group of frontiersmen known as the "Big Knives," took Cahokia, Kaskaskia, and several other British garrisons from British control. Virginia claimed jurisdiction over the region, making it a county of Virginia. However, in 1784, Virginia relinquished its claim on the Illinois region and gave the area to the national government. In 1787, the Northwest Ordinance made the region a part of the Northwest Territory. In 1800, Congress created the Indiana Territory and made the Illinois region part of this area. In 1809, Congress created the Illinois Territory, which included present-day Illinois, most of Wisconsin, and portions of Michigan and Minnesota. The territorial capital was Kaskaskia.

The territorial governments obtained land from Native Americans through a series of treaties which exchanged land for yearly grants of money and other gifts. However, many of the natives in the Illinois Territory were not satisfied with the land agreements and were angered by the continued seizure of their land by the Illinois settlers. As a result, they allied themselves with Britain against America during the War of 1812.

In August 1812, a group of 500 Potawatomi Indians and allied Indians destroyed Fort Dearborn, located at the mouth of the Chicago River, killing both troops and settlers, and burning the fort. The war ended in 1815.

Illinois During the 19th Century

On December 3, 1818, Illinois became the 21st state of the United States. The capital of the new state was Kaskaskia and the first governor was Shadrach Bond, a Democratic-Republican. The population of the new state of Illinois was 34,620. The capital was changed to Vandalia in 1820. This was a temporary measure, meant to last no more than twenty years, and was done to promote land sales and encourage the development of the interior of the state, which was largely uninhabited. In 1839, the state capital was moved permanently to Springfield, IL.

In the mid-1820s, the northern area of Illinois began to be settled. In 1825, the opening of the Erie Canal encouraged more settlers from the northeastern states to move to central and northern Illinois. Settlers from the southern states continued to move to southern Illinois. The state's population increased from 55,211 in 1820 to 157,445 in 1830.

The first state prison, at Alton, was built in 1830. European immigration also increased significantly in the 1830s. By 1830, most Native Americans in Illinois had signed treaties ceding their land and have been forced to move west across the Mississippi River. However, one Sauk chief, Black Hawk, claimed that the Indians had been tricked into signing the agreement and repudiated it. After a peaceful emissary sent by Black Hawk was shot by white settlers in 1832, the Black Hawk War broke out. After an early victory, the Sauk were defeated in late July and were almost completely slaughtered during the Bad Axe Massacre on August 3, 1832. The remaining members of the Sauk were moved to a reservation near Fort Des Moines. The following year, the last treaty with Illinois natives was negotiated, marking the end of Indian-held lands in Illinois. The ending of the war encouraged additional white settlers to come to Illinois and by 1850, the state's population had risen to 851,470.

In 1839, the city of Nauvoo was founded by members of the Church of Jesus Christ of Latter-Day Saints (Mormons) and by 1845, the city had a population of over 12,000. However, the Mormon and non-Mormon population of the area disagreed over various Mormon religious practices, especially that of polygamy. Hostility between the groups increased, especially after Joseph Smith, the leader of the Mormons, announced in 1844 that he would run for President. A group of dissenting Mormons began publishing a newspaper that attacked both Smith's leadership of the Mormons as well as the practice of polygamy. After Smith ordered the press destroyed he was arrested and later killed by a mob who stormed the jail where he was being held. In 1846, the Mormons left the city of Nauvoo and, led by Brigham Young, eventually settled in Utah.

Slavery and its extension to new states and territories was a major issue in Illinois in the 1850s. Many of the settlers in the southern part of the state, who had come from the South, were sympathetic to the pro-slavery movement. However, the northern part of the state, which had been settled by individuals from the Northeast, was primarily opposed to slavery.

In 1858, seven debates on the topic of the extension of slavery were held in Illinois between Abraham Lincoln, a Republican, and Stephen Douglas, a Democrat, both of whom were campaigning for the United States Senate. These brought national attention to Illinois. Although Lincoln lost the election, he received national recognition for his stand on slavery and he was elected to the office of President of the United States in 1860, with the support of all the non-slave states except New Jersey. Six Southern states seceded following Lincoln's election and the Civil War began in 1861. The majority of Illinois residents favored the Union, as both President Lincoln and General (later President) Ulysses S. Grant were from Illinois. Approximately 260,000 Union soldiers came from the state. In 1865, near the end of the Civil War, Illinois became the first state to ratify the Thirteenth Amendment to the United States Constitution, which abolished slavery.

After the end of the Civil War, the state experienced significant growth in agriculture and industry. The Chicago Union Stock Yards opened in 1865; the city quickly became the largest grain and meat-packing center in the country. However, the Chicago Fire of 1871 destroyed 18,000 buildings in the city's downtown area; losses were estimated at $200 to $300 million. This slowed the rapid growth of the city somewhat.

During the late 19th century, railroad workers, miners, and factory workers throughout the United States became disillusioned with wages, hours, and working conditions, leading to many disputes between labor and management. On May 4, 1886, anarchists organized a labor rally at Chicago's Haymarket Square to protest police behavior against striking workers striking at the McCormick reaper works in Chicago. When the police attempted to break up the rally, a bomb was thrown, killing seven police officers and one civilian. In the riot that followed the bombing, gunfire between police and crowd members wounded many police and spectators. The riot led to increased anti-labor sentiment throughout the United States, temporarily weakening support for the labor movement.

Illinois During the 20th Century

During the period of national reform in the late 19th and early 20th century, Illinois became recognized as one of the most progressive states in the country. In 1899, the first juvenile court in the United States was organized in Chicago. In 1903, Illinois was the first state to pass laws establishing an eight-hour workday and limiting children to 48 hours of work per week. In 1909, a law limited the workday for women to ten hours. Labor-management relations began to improve, especially after the publication of Upton Sinclair's *The Jungle*, in 1906. In 1911, Illinois passed a law which authorized payments from public state funds to poor parents for the care of their children; this was the first such statewide law in the country. The state also passed a state workers' compensation act that same year.

The early 20th century also saw the arrival in Illinois of many African Americans from the Deep South. Approximately two-thirds settled in Bronzeville, a district of Chicago. In 1908 a race riot in Springfield led to the founding of the National Association for the Advancement of Colored People (NAACP). Other race riots occurred in East St. Louis in 1917 and in Chicago in 1919, bringing national attention to the state. The Chicago riot, which was the worst race riot in the country, resulted in 38 deaths and 537 injured, as well as leaving approximately 1,000 black families in the city homeless.

In 1917, the United States entered World War I. Illinois was one of only four states which provided enough men to set up an entire Army division, the 33rd or Prairie Division. This was in addition to many other servicemen from Illinois who fought in the war. Over 5,000 Army officers were trained at Fort Sheridan and approximately 125,000 Naval recruits trained at the Great Lakes Naval Training Center.

After the passage of the 18th Amendment in 1919, prohibiting the sale and manufacture of alcohol, Chicago became a hotbed of crime and violence, thanks to gang warfare between Al Capone and rival gangs. The city was also well known for bootlegging. This culminated in the 1929 St. Valentine's Day Massacre, in which Al Capone's gunmen allegedly murdered seven members of the rival Bugs Moran Gang.

During the 1930's the Great Depression led to a decline in manufacturing, resulting in the loss of thousands of jobs. Special sessions of the state legislature were called in 1932 to establish emergency funds for unemployment relief. During that year, the number of unemployed workers in Chicago reached 750,000. In 1933 and 1934, in the middle of the depression, the Century of Progress International Exposition was held in Chicago, to commemorate the centennial of the city's incorporation. The Exposition was extremely successful and helped many businesses in the area from going bankrupt during that period. In 1937, oil fields were discovered in the southeastern part of the state; by 1939, Illinois was the fourth-largest oil-producing state in the country. Chicago Mayor Anton J. Cermak was killed in 1933 in Miami, FL, during an assassination attempt on President-elect Franklin D. Roosevelt.

Illinois became prominent during World War II, not only for its thousands of war plants, but for the research conducted at the University of Chicago by Nobel Prize winner Enrico Fermi and his colleagues, who achieved the first self-sustaining nuclear reaction. This was a major step forward in the development of the atomic bomb. During the 1950s, the Argonne National Laboratory, located near Chicago, became the major research center for the study of industrial uses of nuclear energy. In 1957, the first nuclear power generating station in the country was activated at the Laboratory. The state also became the country's largest producer of steel by 1960. Another noteworthy event was the opening of the first of Raymond Kroc's chain of McDonald's fast food restaurants in Des

Plaines in 1954. During the 1960s, Illinois expanded existing industries, such as chemical and steel manufacture, and developed new ones, including automobile and tire plants.

The Illinois constitution requires that the state legislature be reapportioned every ten years to provide equal representation based upon state population. In 1963, the Democrat and Republican factions in the state legislature could not come to an agreement on a reapportionment plan. In 1964, the General Assembly suspended all districts and authorized an at-large election of 177 members of the state's House of Representatives. After the legislature again failed to agree on a reapportionment plan in 1965, a panel of judges reapportioned the Senate and a special commission reapportioned the House.

In 1964, the state constitution was amended to create a more streamlined and efficient state court system. All lower courts were abolished and the system included three types of courts: circuit courts, appellate courts, and a supreme court. State income taxes were approved by the legislature in 1969. The following year, 1970, voters adopted the first new state constitution since 1870. The constitution went into effect in 1971. A state lottery was adopted in 1973 to raise revenue for a variety of services, including education. In 1977, the General Assembly reinstated capital punishment for adults convicted of any of sixteen categories of murder.

Although the population of Illinois continued to increase between 1950 and 1980, the rate of increase declined. Much of this was due to an economic decline beginning in the 1960s. Economic recovery plans included offering economic incentives to domestic and foreign manufactures to relocate to or remain in the state. In the 1980s and 1990s, high-technology industries in Illinois experienced significant growth. By the 1990s, the state economy had recovered; the unemployment rate in 1996 was just over 5 percent, the lowest rate since 1974.

ILLINOIS TODAY

Illinois is ranked 25th in size in the country, with a total area of 56,343 square miles, including 750 square miles of inland water but not including 1,575 square miles of Great Lakes water over which the state has jurisdiction. The mean elevation is approximately 600 feet. The state has 63 miles of shoreline on Lake Michigan, with several artificial harbors placed along the lakefront. There are no large natural harbors in the state.

According to the 1990 census, Illinois is the sixth most populous state in the country. The census reported a total population of 11,466,682, an increase of less than 1 percent over the 1980 census figure. The 1998 population estimate was 12,045,326. The most populous city in the state is Chicago, with a population of 2,783,726 in 1990. Other large cities with a population over 100,000 include Rockford, Peoria, and Springfield.

In 1990, approximately 85 percent of the state's population lived in urban areas, meaning that they live in or near cities and towns with a population of 2,500 or more. Approximately two-thirds live in the Chicago metropolitan area, which includes approximately 170 incorporated villages, towns, and cities.

Over 90 percent of the state's population were born in the United States. Of those born outside the United States, approximately 30 percent are Mexican and 10 percent are from Poland. Most of the individuals born outside the United States live in the Chicago area. According to the 1990 census, approximately 78 percent of the state's population are white, 15 percent African American, and 8 percent are Hispanic. Nearly two-thirds of the African Americans in Illinois live in Chicago, where they comprise almost 40 percent of the city's population.

Illinois' largest single source of income is service industries; they account for the largest portion of the gross state product. The leading service industries in Illinois include community, business, and personal services as well as finance, insurance, and real estate. Chicago is considered to be the financial capital of the Midwest United States.

Manufacturing is another important economic activity, especially in the Chicago area. The Chicago area is the one of the highest-ranked manufacturing region in the United States, second only to the Los Angeles area. The leading manufactured product in the state is processed foods; other key products include machinery, chemicals, fabricated metal products, printed materials, and electrical equipment.

Tourism is also big business in Illinois, contributing approximately $16 dollars annually.

Illinois has a total of 102 counties. The state elects two United States Senators and 20 members of the House of Representatives, for a total of 22 electoral votes. The current state constitution was adopted in 1970.

CHAPTER 2

INTRODUCTION TO ILLINOIS CRIMINAL LAW

THE STRUCTURE OF THE GOVERNMENT

Illinois criminal law is found in the state constitution and in the Illinois Criminal Code. Both have been frequently modified, amended, and altered.

The first **Illinois Constitution** was ratified in 1818, when Illinois became a state. New constitutions were adopted in 1848 and 1870. The 1870 constitution remained in effect for 100 years, until the state's fourth and present constitution was adopted in 1970 and came into effect in 1971. Unlike the constitution of 1870, which was designed for the primarily agrarian society found in Illinois at that time, the current constitution focuses on the needs and concerns of an industrialized state. The Illinois Constitution is the primary law of the state, although it is of course subordinate to the United States Constitution. No criminal law or constitutional amendment enacted in Illinois may conflict with or violate any individual rights which are guaranteed by the U.S. Constitution, the Bill of Rights, any other Constitutional Amendments, or any federal laws. If any part of the Illinois constitution or legal code is found to be in conflict with the U.S. Constitution or federal statutes, the Illinois enactment is unconstitutional and must be changed. See Schmalleger (p.121) for a discussion of the U.S. Constitution.

There are several ways in which the constitution may be amended or revised, These are described in Article XIV of the Illinois Constitution. First, a new amendment or revision may be proposed by three-fifths of the total membership of each house of the state legislature, which is known as the **Illinois General Assembly**. Second, a **constitutional convention** may be called by the legislature and approved by the voters. In addition, amendments to Article IV of the Constitution, which deals with the legislature, may be proposed through **initiative**, which involves state voters presenting a petition which has been signed by a specified number of voters.

In all cases, any proposed amendment must be placed on the ballot at the next upcoming general election. If the amendment was introduced by the state legislature or by initiative, it must be approved by three-fifths of those voting on it, or a majority of those voting in the election. An amendment that was introduced by a constitutional convention needs to be approved by a majority of those voting on the question.

Like most states, Florida has three branches of government: executive, legislative, and judicial. This is specified in Article II of the Illinois Constitution, which also provides for separation of powers.

The Executive Branch

Article V of the Illinois Constitution discusses the state's **executive branch**, which consists of a governor, lieutenant governor, attorney general, secretary of state, comptroller, and treasurer. They are all elected officers who serve four-year terms which begin on the second Monday of January following their election to office. The governor and lieutenant governor are elected jointly, so that voters cast a single vote for both candidates.

To be elected to an office of the executive branch, candidates must be a United States citizen, be at least 25 years of age, and have been a resident of the state of Illinois for the three years preceding his or her election.

The governor has the supreme executive power in the state. He/she has the power to appoint all officials who are not elected or appointed by some other official. The Governor has the power to veto legislation passed by the state legislature, although a three-fifths majority vote in both houses may override the governor's veto.

On November 3, 1998, George H. Ryan, a Republican, was elected the 39th governor of Illinois. His present term expires in 2003.

The Legislative Branch

The **state legislature** is discussed in Article IV of the Illinois Constitution and is the lawmaking branch of the state government. The Illinois legislature is known as the **General Assembly** and is made up of two houses, a 59-member Senate and a 118-member House of Representatives. The state is divided into 59 Legislative Districts, with one senator elected from each District. Senators serve either two- or four-year terms. Each Legislative District is divided into two Representative Districts and one representative is elected from each Representative District. Representatives all serve two-year terms. All members of the General Assembly are elected at the general election held in even-numbered years. To serve as a member of the General Assembly, a candidate must be a United States citizen, be at least 21 years of age, and have been a resident of the district he or she is to represent for the two years prior to election or appointment.

The General Assembly meets annually on the second Wednesday of January. In addition, the governor may call a special session of the General Assembly or of the Senate alone. Special sessions of the General Assembly may also be called jointly by the presiding officers of both houses.

Each house selects its own officers from among its membership during an election held on the first day of the January session in odd-numbered years. The presiding officer of the Senate is known as the President of the Senate and the presiding officer of the House of Representatives is known as the Speaker of the House of Representatives.

The Judicial Branch

The judicial branch of the government, which is discussed in Article VI of the Illinois Constitution, contains the various Illinois courts. These include a state supreme court, appellate courts, and circuit courts. The state is divided into five Judicial Districts for the purpose of selecting judges for the supreme and appellate courts. The First Judicial District is made up of Cook County, which includes Chicago while the rest of the state is divided up into the other four districts.

The highest court in Illinois is the **Illinois Supreme Court**, which is made up of seven justices, who serve ten-year terms. Three are elected from the First Judicial District and one justice is elected from each of the other four Districts. The judges select one member from amongst themselves to serve as a chief justice, who serves a three-year term. The **Appellate Courts** are the lower courts of appeal. Each Judicial District contains at least one Appellate Division, from which at least three appellate court judges are elected. Like supreme court justices, appellate court judges also serve ten-year terms.

The courts of original jurisdiction in Illinois are known as **Circuit Courts**; these courts have original jurisdiction over all cases except those in which the Supreme Court has original and exclusive jurisdiction. Circuit court judges serve terms of six years. They appoint Associate Judges to serve four-year terms.

To be eligible to serve as a judge or associate judge in Illinois, an individual must be a United States citizen, an attorney licensed in the state, and a resident of the unit (District, Division, or Circuit) which selects him or her.

Passing a Law in Illinois

In Illinois, a bill may be introduced into either the House or the Senate and, after it has been passed by one of the two legislative houses it may still be amended or rejected by the other. For a bill to be passed, it must receive a majority vote in each of the two houses. After both houses have passed a bill, it is presented within thirty calendar days to the governor. The governor has sixty calendar days to veto the bill, which he does by returning it with his objections to the house from which it originated. If the governor signs the bill, or fails to return it within the sixty-day period, the bill becomes law. The legislature may, by a three-fifths vote of each house, enact a bill into law over the governor's veto.

Local Government in Illinois

Local government in Illinois is discussed in Article VII of the constitution. Each of the 102 counties in Illinois has an elected county board. The number of members of the board is determined by county ordinance. Some counties elect a chief executive but the majority appoint a county administrator, All counties are required by Article VII, §4 of the constitution to elect a sheriff, a treasurer, and a county clear. They have the option of electing other officers as well, including a coroner, recorder, assessor, and auditor.

Article VII, §6 of the Constitution provides the right of **home rule** to counties that have an elected chief executive officer and any municipalities with a population of over 25,000. In addition, smaller municipalities may elect by referendum to become a home rule unit. The rights under home rule include local control of governmental services such as emergency services. This means, for example, that any home rule unit may set up its own local police department. Counties and municipalities that are not home rule units are limited to those powers which the constitution and the law specifically grants to them.

THE CRIMINAL LAW IN ILLINOIS

There are several sources of criminal law in Illinois (see Schmalleger, pp.119-123 for a discussion of the development of law). These include:

- federal and state constitutions
- statutory criminal law
- case law

Together, the Illinois State Constitution and the U.S. Constitution provide the basic framework for criminal law, first by focusing on individual rights and on the limitations placed on government power and second by requiring the establishment of a judicial system. However, neither the federal nor the state constitution significantly emphasizes the creation or definition of crimes.

The primary source of **statutory criminal law** in Illinois is the Illinois Criminal Code, which is codified in Chapter 720 of the Illinois Compiled Statutes (ILCS). However, other statutes also contain laws which relate to crime and punishment. For example, Chapter 725 of the Illinois Statutes, which is entitled "Criminal Procedure," contains laws relating to procedures such as arrests, trial, and sentencing. Chapter 730, entitled "Corrections," contains laws relating to offender sanctions. See Schmalleger (pp.127-128) for a discussion of criminal law.

Statutory citations from the ILCS include the number of the chapter, act, and section and may appear complicated at first glance. A sample statutory citation is **720 ILCS 5/9-2**. 720 refers to the chapter of the statutes, which in this case is the chapter on criminal offenses. ILCS stands for Illinois Compiled Statutes. The number 5 refers to Act 5 of the chapter, which is the Criminal Code of 1961. The number 9 refers to Article 9 of this Act, which discusses Homicide. Finally, the number 2 refers to section 2 of Article 9. Thus, the entire citation, 720 ILCS 5/9-2 refers to the specific statute which defines second degree murder.

The Illinois Criminal Code was originally based on the English **common law** (see Schmalleger, pp.120-121), which became the law of the original thirteen colonies and then evolved into the law of the individual states as they entered the union. However, 720 ILCS 5/1-3, which discusses the applicability of common law, states that:

> No conduct constitutes an offense unless it is described as an offense in this Code or in another statute of this State. However, this provision does not affect the power of a court to punish for contempt or to employ any sanction authorized by law for the enforcement of an order or civil judgment.

Case law (see Schmalleger, p.133) consists of appellate court decisions or opinions which interpret the meaning of the law. Effectively, case law is made by judges when they hand down decisions in court. Because of the principle of *stare decisis*, or precedent (see Schmalleger, p.133), a decision made by a judge in one court will be followed by later judges in the state until the same court reverses its decision or until the decision is overturned by a higher court.

The Illinois Criminal Code contains two types of law, substantive and procedural. Schmalleger (see p.128) defines **substantive criminal law** as "that part of the law that defines crimes and specifies punishments." Article 9, which is the section of the Criminal Code that discusses and defines homicide is an example of substantive criminal law. **Procedural law**, on the other hand, is defined by Schmalleger (see p.133) as "the aspect of the law that specifies the methods to be used in enforcing substantive law." In other words, procedural law outlines the rules that the state must follow when dealing with crimes and criminals. These include the procedures that must be used to investigate crimes, arrest suspects, and carry out formal prosecution. The right to a speedy trial, which is discussed in 725 ILCS 5/103-5, is an example of procedural law.

THE DEFINITION AND CLASSIFICATION OF CRIME

Schmalleger (see pp.134-136) discusses the varies types or categories of violations of the criminal law. In Illinois, an **offense** is defined in 720 ILCS 5/2-12 simply as "a violation of any penal statute of this State." Note that Schmalleger (p.135) uses this term differently than the ILCS; in the text, it refers specifically to minor violations of the criminal law, rather than to crime in general.

Illinois recognized two main categories of crimes, felonies and misdemeanors. Each category is broken down into classes which define the level of seriousness of the offense. **Felonies** (see Schmalleger, p.134) are the most serious offenses in Illinois. 720 ILCS 5/2-7 defines a felony as:

> an offense for which a sentence to death or to a term of imprisonment in a penitentiary for one year or more is provided.

In addition, according to 720 ILCS 5/2-8 certain serious felonies are considered to be **forcible felonies**. These include:

> treason, first degree murder, second degree murder, predatory criminal sexual assault of a child, aggravated criminal sexual assault, criminal sexual assault, robbery, burglary, residential burglary, aggravated arson, arson, aggravated kidnaping, kidnaping, aggravated battery resulting in great bodily harm or permanent disability or disfigurement and any other felony which involves the use or threat of physical force or violence against any individual.

A **misdemeanor** (see Schmalleger, p.134) is defined in 720 ILCS 5/2-11 as:

> any offense for which a sentence to a term of imprisonment in other than a penitentiary for less than one year may be imposed.

Thus, in Illinois, the difference between a felony and a misdemeanor is not determined by the offense itself, or by the action committed by the offender, but by the possible punishment that is prescribed in the Criminal Code. Even if the Criminal Code does not specifically identify a crime as a misdemeanor or a felony, the classification can easily be inferred from the prescribed sentence.

Offenders convicted of felonies and misdemeanor offenses may be sentenced to pay a fine as well as to a term of imprisonment. 730 ILCS 5/5-9-1 outlines the fines for each classification of crime. For example, offenders found guilty of felony offenses may be sentenced to a fine of $25,000, or the specific amount specified in the offense statute, whichever is greater.

Schmalleger (p.135) also reviews a specific category of crime known as **treason**. In Illinois, treason is defined in 720 ILCS 5/30-1 as:

> (a) A person owing allegiance to this State commits treason when he or she knowingly:
> (1) Levies war against this State; or
> (2) Adheres to the enemies of this State, giving them aid or comfort.
> (b) No person may be convicted of treason except on the testimony of 2 witnesses to the same overt act, or on his confession in open court.
> (c) Sentence. Treason is a Class X felony for which an offender may be sentenced to death under Section 5-5-3 of the Unified Code of Corrections.

Illinois also recognizes a crime called **misprison of treason**, which is discussed in 720 ILCS 5/30-2 and involves having knowledge of an act of treason and failing to report it to one of the individuals specified in the statute. Misprison of treason is a Class 4 felony in Illinois.

Schmalleger (see p.135-136) also discusses the concept of **inchoate offenses**. He defines an inchoate offense as: "An offense not yet completed. Also, an offense that consists of an action or conduct that is a step toward the intended commission of another offense." Illinois recognizes three types of inchoate offenses, which are discussed in 720 ILCS 5/8. **Solicitation** is defined in 720 ILCS 5/8-1 as:

> A person commits solicitation when, with intent that an offense be committed, other than first degree murder, he commands, encourages or requests another to commit that offense.

The statute also defines the penalty for solicitation, which may include either a fine or imprisonment or both, but may not exceed the maximum penalty which is provided for the offense that was solicited. In addition, separate sections of the ILCS (720 ILCS 5/8-1.1 and 720 ILCS 5/8-1.2) discuss the specific offenses of solicitation of murder and solicitation of murder for hire. **Conspiracy**, which is outlined in 720 ILCS 5/8-2, is defined as:

> A person commits conspiracy when, with intent that an offense be committed, he agrees with another to the commission of that offense. No person may be convicted of conspiracy to commit an offense unless an act in furtherance of such agreement is alleged and proved to have been committed by him or by a co-conspirator.

As with criminal solicitation, the seriousness of the sanction depends on the nature of the intended crime. The third type of inchoate offense is **attempt**. This crime is defined in 720 ILCS 5/8-4, which states that:

> A person commits an attempt when, with intent to commit a specific offense, he does
> any act which constitutes a substantial step toward the commission of that offense.

The statute also states that an accused individual may not use as a defense to a charge of attempt the claim that it would in actuality have been impossible for the accused to commit the attempted offense.

Schmalleger (see pp.122-123) discusses the distinction between *mala in se* and *mala prohibita* crimes. These terms, which date back to the common law, relate to the seriousness of an offense. *Mala in se* crimes involve behaviors that are considered to be inherently wrong or evil in and of themselves. Murder, rape, arson, and incest are examples of *mala in se* crimes. *Mala prohibita* crimes are behaviors that are wrong only because they have been forbidden by legislative act, not because they are considered to be inherently evil. Examples of *mala prohibita* crimes include traffic violations and drug use. However, these terms are not found in the Illinois Criminal Code.

The Criminal Act (*Actus Reus*) and Intent (*Mens Rea*)

Schmalleger (see pp.136-140) discusses the general features of crime. On p.136, he defines the **criminal act (*actus reus*)** as "an act in violation of the law." In Illinois, 720 ILCS 5/4-1 states that:

> A material element of every offense is a voluntary act, which includes an omission
> to perform a duty which the law imposes on the offender and which he is physically
> capable of performing.

Most criminal acts are deliberate and voluntary on the part of the offender. However, the act necessary to make up a crime will vary with each crime. Verbal actions (words) can be a sufficient action in, for example, the crime of perjury. Merely possessing something may be a sufficient act if the crime is one that involves illegal possession of goods (see 720 ILCS 5/4-2).

It is clear from the statute that the criminal act may also consist of some form of passive participation or omission or failure to act. An **omission** occurs when someone who has a legal duty to act fails to perform an action that is required by law. For example, a security guard who deliberately looks the other way while company property is stolen is a passive participant and is guilty of omission to act. Similarly, a parent or other legal caretaker who fails to adequately feed and shelter an infant, resulting in the death of the child, may have committed a crime by his or her failure to act.

Failing to act is only a crime of omission when an individual has a legal duty to act in that situation and when the individual is physically able to perform that duty. For example, consider the case of a swimmer at a local public pool who develops a cramp while in deep water. The lifeguard who is on duty at the pool has a legal duty to act and, if he/she fails to go to the swimmer's assistance, would be guilty of a crime of omission. However, the other swimmers in the pool have only a moral duty to aid the distressed swimmer and if they fail to provide assistance would not be guilty of any crime. In addition, the omission or failure to act must also be voluntary for this statute to apply.

Schmalleger (see p.137) defines the **guilty mind (*mens rea*)** as "the state of mind that accompanies a criminal act." In Illinois, mental state is discussed in 720 ILCS 5/4-3, which states that:

(a) A person is not guilty of an offense, other than an offense which involves absolute liability, unless, with respect to each element described by the statute defining the offense, he acts while having one of the mental states described in Sections 4--4 through 4--7.
(b) If the statute defining an offense prescribed a particular mental state with respect to the offense as a whole, without distinguishing among the elements thereof, the prescribed mental state applies to each such element. If the statute does not prescribe a particular mental state applicable to an element of an offense (other than an offense which involves absolute liability), any mental state defined in Sections 4--4, 4--5 or 4--6 is applicable.
(c) Knowledge that certain conduct constitutes an offense, or knowledge of the existence, meaning, or application of the statute defining an offense, is not an element of the offense unless the statute clearly defines it as such.

Effectively, for an individual to have mens rea in Illinois, the crime must have been committed intentionally, knowingly, recklessly, or with criminal negligence; these terms are defined in 720 ILCS 7/4-4 through 7/4-7. A crime is committed **intentionally** (see Schmalleger, p.137) when the offender consciously desires the outcome or consciously desires to engage in the behavior described by the statute that defines the offense. A crime is committed **knowingly** (see Schmalleger, p.137) when the offender is aware that his or her conduct violates the law. A crime is committed **recklessly** (see Schmalleger, p.137) when the offender is aware of the risk of his or her actions and consciously disregards that risk. Finally, **negligence** (see Schmalleger, p.137) occurs when the offender fails to perceive a substantial and unjustifiable risk that would be perceived by any reasonable person.

Strict liability offenses (see Schmalleger, p.138) are crimes for which a culpable mental state, or *mens rea*, does not have to be shown. In Illinois, this is known as **absolute liability**. In these situations, the offender may be punished without proof of criminal intent. Absolute liability crimes arerare; 720 ILCS 5/4-9 states that they only occur if the crime is a misdemeanor which is not punishable by incarceration or by a fine exceeding $500, or if the statute that defines the offense specifically outlines the imposition of absolute liability.

DEFENSES TO A CRIMINAL CHARGE

Schmalleger (pp.143-160) discusses in detail the topic of defenses to a criminal charge, outlining several specific categories of defenses. Many of these defenses are specifically mentioned in the Illinois criminal code.

Justifications

Schmalleger (p.143) defines **justification** as "a legal defense in which the defendant admits committing the act in question but claims it was necessary to avoid some greater evil." The issue of **justifiable use of force** is discussed in Act 5, Article 7 of the criminal code. This includes self defense, defense of others, and defense of home and property. 720 ILCS 5/7-1 discusses the use of force in the defense of a person, stating that:

> A person is justified in the use of force against another when and to the extent that he reasonably believes that such conduct is necessary to defend himself or another against such other's imminent use of unlawful force. However, he is justified in the use of force which is intended or likely to cause death or great bodily harm only if he reasonably believes that such force is necessary to prevent imminent death or great bodily harm to himself or another, or the commission of a forcible felony.

This statute relates to both **self defense** (see Schmalleger, p.144), in which the defendant claims that the use of force against the victim was justifiable because it was the only way the defendant could ensure his/her own safety, and **defense of others** (see Schmalleger, pp.144-145), in which the defendant claims that the use of force was needed to protect a third person. It is clear from this statute that the amount of force used must be proportionate to the amount of force or threat that the defendant is experiencing. The statute states that **deadly force** (see Schmalleger, p.144) may only be used if the defendant believes that he/she or another person is in imminent danger of death or great bodily harm or to prevent the other party from committing a forcible felony (which could result in death or great bodily harm to someone).

Schmalleger (p.145) also discusses the issue of **defense of home and property**, which is covered in 720 ILCS 5/7-2 and 5/7-3. The first section (5/7-2) deals specifically with the use of force in defending a dwelling place and states that:

> A person is justified in the use of force against another when and to the extent that he reasonably believes that such conduct is necessary to prevent or terminate such other's unlawful entry into or attack upon a dwelling. However, he is justified in the use of force which is intended or likely to cause death or great bodily harm only if:
> (a) The entry is made or attempted in a violent, riotous, or tumultuous manner, and he reasonably believes that such force is necessary to prevent an assault upon, or offer of personal violence to, him or another then in the dwelling, or
> (b) He reasonably believes that such force is necessary to prevent the commission of a felony in the dwelling.

The second statute (5/7-3) is similar but applies to real property that is not a dwelling and to personal property which is in the individual's possession or control.

Another justification defense discussed in Schmalleger is that of **necessity** (see p.145). This defense, which is defined in 720 ILCS 5/7-14, claims that commission of the offense of which the defendant is accused was necessary to prevent even greater harm from occurring.

Schmalleger also discusses the justification defense of **consent** (see p.146). This defense claims that the injured person consented to the actions that caused the injury. This defense seems to be most commonly used in sex-related offenses, such as sexual battery. For example, 720 ILCS 5/12-17 defines consent in certain crimes of criminal sexual assault as:

> "Consent" means a freely given agreement to the act of sexual penetration or sexual conduct in question. Lack of verbal or physical resistance or submission by the victim resulting from the use of force or threat of force by the accused shall not constitute

consent. The manner of dress of the victim at the time of the offense shall not constitute consent.

The statute makes it clear that coerced consent, obtained through threats of force or violence against the victim or another person, does not constitute a defense of consent.

Excuses

Schmalleger (p.143) defines an **excuse** as:

> a legal defense in which the defendant claims that some personal condition or circumstance at the time of the act was such that he or she should not be held accountable under the criminal law.

The category of excuses is discussed in Schmalleger on pp.146-152. Probably the most well-known (and controversial) defense in this category is that of **insanity** (see Schmalleger, pp.148-152). Although the term insanity is no longer used by mental health professionals, it is a legal term referring to a defense that is based on the defendant's claim that he/she was mentally ill or mentally incapacitated at the time of the offense.

In Illinois, insanity is discussed in 720 ILCS 5/6-2. The statute states that:

> (a) A person is not criminally responsible for conduct if at the time of such conduct, as a result of mental disease or mental defect, he lacks substantial capacity to appreciate the criminality of his conduct.

It is clear from this section of the statute that Illinois uses the **substantial capacity test** for insanity (see Schmalleger, p.149).

When the defense of insanity is presented, the burden of proof is on the defendant to prove that he/she lacks substantial capacity to appreciate the criminality of his/her conduct. If the defendant is acquitted of criminal charges using the insanity defense, he/she will be found **not guilty by reason of insanity**. Illinois also recognizes the verdict of **guilty but mentally ill** (see Schmalleger, pp.150-151); 720 ILCS 5/6-2(c) states that:

> c) A person who, at the time of the commission of a criminal offense, was not insane but was suffering from a mental illness, is not relieved of criminal responsibility for his conduct and may be found guilty but mentally ill.

Mental illness is defined to be a disorder of behavior, thought, or mood that impairs the judgment of the defendant but not enough so that the defendant is unable to appreciate the wrongfulness of his/her behavior.

Another defense that falls into the category of excuses is that of **duress** (see Schmalleger, p.146). In Illinois, this defense is known as **compulsion** and is defined in 720 ILCS 5/7-11. Effectively, if the defendant commits a crime under some type of threat of imminent death or great bodily harm, he/she is not guilty of the offense. However, the statute provides for one exception: compulsion may not be used as a defense to an offense that is punishable by death.

The defense of **age** or **infancy** (see Schmalleger, pp.146-147) also falls into this category. 720 ILCS 5/6-1 states that:

> No person shall be convicted of any offense unless he had attained his 13th birthday at the time the offense was committed.

Schmalleger (see pp.147-148) also discusses the excuse defense of **involuntary intoxication** (see Schmalleger, pp.147-148). In Illinois, if an individual is drugged or intoxicated, he/she is criminally responsible for his/her behavior. However, according to 720 ILCS 5/6-3, there are two exceptions to this; one of these applies if the intoxication or drugged condition was produced involuntarily.

Schmalleger (see p.147) discusses the defense of **mistake**, including both **mistake of law** and **mistake of fact**. While in most cases, the old saying that "ignorance of the law is no defense" is true, there are some exceptions. 720 ILCS 5/4-8 states that ignorance or mistake of fact or law may be a defense if knowledge is not a required element of the offense or if the ignorance or mistake negates the existence of the required mental state. According to the statute, the individual's reasonable belief that his or her behavior is not a crime is a defense in four specific situations:

- the offense is defined in an administrative regulation which has not been published and could not be reasonably known to the individual;

- the individual is relying on a statute which is later determined to be invalid;

- the individual is relying on a court order or opinion which was later overruled by a higher court;

- the individual is relying on an interpretation of a statute which was issued by an official agency that has been empowered to interpret that statute.

Procedural Defenses

Schmalleger (see p.143) defines a **procedural defense** as:

> A defense which claims that the defendant was in some significant way discriminated against in the justice process or that some important aspect of official procedure was not properly followed in the investigation or prosecution of the crime charged.

Schmalleger discusses the topic of procedural defenses on pp.152-155. Effectively, these defenses claim that some form of procedural law was not properly followed. One of the defenses covered in Schmalleger (see p.155) is the **denial of a speedy trial**. In Illinois, the right to a speedy trial is guaranteed in Article I, Section 8 of the Illinois State Constitution as well as in 725 ILCS 103-5. The time limit for a trial to be "speedy" is, in most cases, 120 to 160 days. This time limit may be extended under certain circumstances. Obviously, if the defendant has requested an extension, he/she may not later claim that his/her right to a speedy trial was denied. However, if the time limit has not been extended by request and if there are no exceptional circumstances which caused a delay, the statute states that the individual must be discharged from custody or released from the obligations of bail or recognizance.

Another issue is that of **double jeopardy** (see Schmalleger, pp.153-154). Article I, Section 10 of the Illinois State Constitution states that:

> No person shall be compelled in a criminal case to give evidence against himself nor be twice put in jeopardy for the same offense.

Similarly, 720 ILCS 5/3-4 states that:

> (a) A prosecution is barred if the defendant was formerly prosecuted for the same offense, based upon the same facts, if such former prosecution:
>   (1) Resulted in either a conviction or an acquittal or in a determination that the evidence was insufficient to warrant a conviction; or
>   (2) Was terminated by a final order or judgment, even if entered before trial, which required a determination inconsistent with any fact or legal proposition necessary to a conviction in the subsequent prosecution; or
>   (3) Was terminated improperly after the jury was impaneled and sworn or, in a trial before a court without a jury, after the first witness was sworn but before findings were rendered by the trier of facts, or after a plea of guilty was accepted by the court.
> A conviction of an included offense is an acquittal of the offense charged.

Another procedural defense discussed in Schmalleger (see pp.152-153) is **entrapment**. 720 ILCS 5/7-12 discusses the issue of entrapment, stating that:

> A person is not guilty of an offense if his or her conduct is incited or induced by a public officer or employee, or agent of either, for the purpose of obtaining evidence for the prosecution of that person. However, this Section is inapplicable if the person was pre-disposed to commit the offense and the public officer or employee, or agent of either, merely affords to that person the opportunity or facility for committing an offense.

The entrapment defense, which is extremely difficult for the defendant to prove, is most commonly used when the defendant was ensnared in an undercover police action; the most frequent use seems to relate to the sale of illegal drugs. In general, the defendant will claim that he/she does not regularly sell drugs but made a sale as a favor to the undercover officer. One of the most common ways for the police to prevent the use of this defense is to make two or more purchases from the same suspect; after the suspect has made multiple sales, the jury is more likely to believe that the undercover officer simply provided the defendant with an opportunity to commit the crime, rather than that the officer induced or encouraged the defendant to engage in a behavior in which he/she would not normally become involved.

Innovative Defenses

Finally, Schmalleger (see pp.156-160) discusses the topic of **innovative defenses**, which are all relatively new and novel defenses against conviction. However, these defenses are not specifically discussed in the Illinois Criminal Code.

CHAPTER 3

INDEX CRIMES

INTRODUCTION

The Federal Bureau of Investigation annually publishes the *Uniform Crime Reports* (UCR), the most widely-used source of official data on crime and criminals in the United States. Schmalleger (see pp.33-53) discusses the UCR in detail. Much of the UCR deals with **index crimes**, a set of eight serious offenses that the FBI uses as a measure of crime in the United States. They are also known as **Part I Offenses**. Four of them are violent crimes; the other four are property crimes. The eight index crimes measured by the FBI are:

- homicide
- forcible rape
- robbery
- aggravated assault
- burglary
- larceny-theft
- motor-vehicle theft
- arson

However, the definitions used by the FBI in compiling the UCR are not always the same as those found in the Illinois Compiled Statutes. This chapter will discuss the definitions of these eight serious crimes as provided by the Illinois criminal code.

CRIMINAL HOMICIDE

Homicide is the killing of one human being by another. If that killing is illegal, then it is a form of **criminal homicide**. Schmalleger discusses the crime of criminal homicide, or murder, on pp.40-41 and on pp.140-142. In Illinois, homicide is discussed in 720 ILCS 5/9 and includes the crimes of first degree murder, second degree murder, and manslaughter.

First Degree Murder

Schmalleger specifically discusses **first degree murder** on pp. 140-141. The crime is discussed in 720 ILCS 5/9-1, which states that:

> (a) A person who kills an individual without lawful justification commits first degree murder if, in performing the acts which cause the death:

> (1) he either intends to kill or do great bodily harm to that individual or another, or knows that such acts will cause death to that individual or another; or
> (2) he knows that such acts create a strong probability of death or great bodily harm to that individual or another; or
> (3) he is attempting or committing a forcible felony other than second degree murder.

This statute identifies two specific categories of first degree murder: **premeditated murder** and **felony murder**. The first category (discussed in sections a1 and a2) involves the intentional killing of another person, although the law does not define the amount of time that must pass between forming the premeditated idea of killing and the actual killing itself. It merely requires that the intent to kill be formed before the killing takes place. On the other hand, felony murder (discussed in section a3) does not require proof of premeditated intent to kill. It merely requires that the offender was engaged in one of a specified list of crimes and that death occurred as a consequence of and while the offender was committing that crime.

Murder in the first degree is a capital felony in Illinois. According to 730 ILCS 5/5-5-3,

> (c)(1) When a defendant is found guilty of first degree murder the State may either seek a sentence of imprisonment ... or where appropriate seek a sentence of death under Section 9-1 of the Criminal Code of 1961.

The statute also states that for the crime of first degree murder, if a sentence of death is not imposed, the offender may not be sentenced to a period of probation, a term of periodic imprisonment, or conditional discharge.

720 ILCS 5/9-1 discusses the proceedings for determining the sentence in a case of first degree murder. After the defendant has been found guilty of the crime, a separate sentencing proceeding must be held to determine whether the sentence will be death or life imprisonment. The hearing may be held before the same jury that determined guilt or innocence or before a new jury impaneled for the sentencing hearing or, if the defendant waives the sentencing jury, by the court alone, with no jury present. To be sentenced to death, the court or jury must find:

1. that the defendant was at least 18 years of age at the time the offense was committed
2. at least one of the aggravating circumstances outlined in the statute exist.

The statute (720 ILCS 5/9-1(b)) lists 20 aggravating circumstances which may be considered by the court and/or jury when determining the sentence in a case of first degree murder, although the court or jury is not limited to these factors. These factors include:

(1) the murdered individual was a peace officer or fireman killed in the course of performing his official duties, to prevent the performance of his official duties, or in retaliation for performing his official duties, and the defendant knew or should have known that the murdered individual was a peace officer or fireman; or

(2) the murdered individual was an employee of an institution or facility of the Department of Corrections, or any similar local correctional agency, killed in the course of performing his official duties, to prevent the performance of his official duties, or in retaliation for performing his official duties, or the murdered individual was an inmate at such institution or facility and was killed on the grounds thereof, or the murdered individual was otherwise present in such institution or facility with the knowledge and approval of the chief administrative officer thereof; or

(3) the defendant has been convicted of murdering two or more individuals under subsection (a) of this Section or under any law of the United States or of any state which is substantially similar to subsection (a) of this Section regardless of whether the deaths occurred as the result of the same act or of several related or unrelated acts so long as the deaths were the result of either an intent to kill more than one person or of separate acts which the defendant knew would cause death or create a strong probability of death or great bodily harm to the murdered individual or another; or

(4) the murdered individual was killed as a result of the hijacking of an airplane, train, ship, bus or other public conveyance; or

(5) the defendant committed the murder pursuant to a contract, agreement or understanding by which he was to receive money or anything of value in return for committing the murder or procured another to commit the murder for money or anything of value; or

(6) the murdered individual was killed in the course of another felony if:
 (a) the murdered individual:
  (i) was actually killed by the defendant, or
  (ii) received physical injuries personally inflicted by the defendant substantially contemporaneously with physical injuries caused by one or more persons for whose conduct the defendant is legally accountable under Section 5-2 of this Code, and the physical injuries inflicted by either the defendant or the other person or persons for whose conduct he is legally accountable caused the death of the murdered individual; and
 (b) in performing the acts which caused the death of the murdered individual or which resulted in physical injuries personally inflicted by the defendant on the murdered individual under the circumstances of subdivision (ii) of subparagraph (a) of paragraph (6) of subsection (b) of this Section, the defendant acted with the intent to kill the

murdered individual or with the knowledge that his acts created a strong probability of death or great bodily harm to the murdered individual or another; and

 (c) the other felony was one of the following: armed robbery, armed violence, robbery, predatory criminal sexual assault of a child, aggravated criminal sexual assault, aggravated kidnapping, aggravated vehicular hijacking, forcible detention, arson, aggravated arson, aggravated stalking, burglary, residential burglary, home invasion, calculated criminal drug conspiracy ... streetgang criminal drug conspiracy ..., or the attempt to commit any of the felonies listed in this subsection (c); or

(7) the murdered individual was under 12 years of age and the death resulted from exceptionally brutal or heinous behavior indicative of wanton cruelty; or

(8) the defendant committed the murder with intent to prevent the murdered individual from testifying in any criminal prosecution or giving material assistance to the State in any investigation or prosecution, either against the defendant or another; or the defendant committed the murder because the murdered individual was a witness in any prosecution or gave material assistance to the State in any investigation or prosecution, either against the defendant or another; or

(9) the defendant, while committing an offense punishable under Sections 401, 401.1, 401.2, 405, 405.2, 407 or 407.1 or subsection (b) of Section 404 of the Illinois Controlled Substances Act, or while engaged in a conspiracy or solicitation to commit such offense, intentionally killed an individual or counseled, commanded, induced, procured or caused the intentional killing of the murdered individual; or

(10) the defendant was incarcerated in an institution or facility of the Department of Corrections at the time of the murder, and while committing an offense punishable as a felony under Illinois law, or while engaged in a conspiracy or solicitation to commit such offense, intentionally killed an individual or counseled, commanded, induced, procured or caused the intentional killing of the murdered individual; or

(11) the murder was committed in a cold, calculated and premeditated manner pursuant to a preconceived plan, scheme or design to take a human life by unlawful means, and the conduct of the defendant created a reasonable expectation that the death of a human being would result therefrom; or

(12) the murdered individual was an emergency medical technician - ambulance, emergency medical technician - intermediate, emergency medical technician - paramedic, ambulance driver, or other medical assistance or first aid personnel, employed by a municipality or other governmental unit, killed in the course of performing his official duties, to prevent the performance of his official duties, or in retaliation for performing his official duties, and the defendant knew or should have known that the murdered individual was an emergency medical

technician - ambulance, emergency medical technician - intermediate, emergency medical technician - paramedic, ambulance driver, or other medical assistance or first aid personnel; or

(13) the defendant was a principal administrator, organizer, or leader of a calculated criminal drug conspiracy consisting of a hierarchical position of authority superior to that of all other members of the conspiracy, and the defendant counseled, commanded, induced, procured, or caused the intentional killing of the murdered person; or

(14) the murder was intentional and involved the infliction of torture. For the purpose of this Section torture means the infliction of or subjection to extreme physical pain, motivated by an intent to increase or prolong the pain, suffering or agony of the victim; or

(15) the murder was committed as a result of the intentional discharge of a firearm by the defendant from a motor vehicle and the victim was not present within the motor vehicle; or

(16) the murdered individual was 60 years of age or older and the death resulted from exceptionally brutal or heinous behavior indicative of wanton cruelty; or

(17) the murdered individual was a disabled person and the defendant knew or should have known that the murdered individual was disabled...; or

(18) the murder was committed by reason of any person's activity as a community policing volunteer or to prevent any person from engaging in activity as a community policing volunteer; or

(19) the murdered individual was subject to an order of protection and the murder was committed by a person against whom the same order of protection was issued under the Illinois Domestic Violence Act of 1986; or

(20) the murdered individual was known by the defendant to be a teacher or other person employed in any school and the teacher or other employee is upon the grounds of a school or grounds adjacent to a school, or is in any part of a building used for school purposes.

The burden of proof in establishing the existence of aggravating factors is on the State and must be proved beyond a reasonable doubt.

In addition, the statute lists five mitigating circumstances which may also be considered by the jury and the court during the sentencing proceedings. These include but are not limited to:

(1) the defendant has no significant history of prior criminal activity;
(2) the murder was committed while the defendant was under the influence of extreme mental or emotional disturbance, although not such as to constitute a defense to prosecution;
(3) the murdered individual was a participant in the defendant's homicidal conduct or consented to the homicidal act;
(4) the defendant acted under the compulsion of threat or menace of the imminent infliction of death or great bodily harm;

(5) the defendant was not personally present during commission of the act or acts causing death.

If the court or the jury find that none of the aggravating factors exists, then the offender will be sentenced to a term of imprisonment. If one or more aggravating factors are found to exist by the court, or by a unanimous vote of the jury, the court or jury determines whether there are any mitigating factors present that are sufficient to preclude the sentence of death. If they find that the aggravating circumstances are not outweighed by the mitigating circumstances (if any), the court will sentence the offender to death. According to 730 ILCS 5/5-8-1(a)(1), for the crime of first degree murder, if the offender is not sentenced to death, he/she shall be sentenced to a term of imprisonment of not less than 20 years and not more than 60 years or, if any aggravating factors exist, to a term of life imprisonment.

According to 720 ILCS 5/9-1(i),

> The conviction and sentence of death shall be subject to automatic review by the Supreme Court. Such review shall be in accordance with rules promulgated by the Supreme Court.

Second Degree Murder

Schmalleger specifically discusses **second degree murder** on p.141. The crime is discussed in 720 ILCS 5/9-2, which states that:

> (a) A person commits the offense of second degree murder when he commits the offense of first degree murder ... and either of the following mitigating factors are present:
> (1) At the time of the killing he is acting under a sudden and intense passion resulting from serious provocation by the individual killed or another whom the offender endeavors to kill, but he negligently or accidentally causes the death of the individual killed; or
> (2) At the time of the killing he believes the circumstances to be such that, if they existed, would justify or exonerate the killing ..., but his belief is unreasonable.
> (b) Serious provocation is conduct sufficient to excite an intense passion in a reasonable person.

The burden of proof is on the defendant to prove either of the two mitigating factors listed in the statute by a preponderance of the evidence before the defendant can be convicted of second degree murder instead of first degree murder. Second degree murder is a Class 1 felony in Illinois. However, according to 730 ILCS 5/5-8-1(a)(1.5), the term of imprisonment for second degree murder shall be not less than 4 years and not more than 20 years. For all other Class 1 felonies, the maximum term of imprisonment is 15 years.

Involuntary Manslaughter and Reckless Homicide

The crimes of **involuntary manslaughter** and **reckless homicide** are defined in 720 ILCS 5/9-3, which states that:

> (a) A person who unintentionally kills an individual without lawful justification commits involuntary manslaughter if his acts whether lawful or unlawful which cause the death are such as are likely to cause death or great bodily harm to some individual, and he performs them recklessly, except in cases in which the cause of the death consists of the driving of a motor vehicle or operating a snowmobile, all-terrain vehicle, or watercraft, in which case the person commits reckless homicide.

Effectively, based on this statute, the crime of manslaughter becomes that of reckless homicide if the death occurred while the offender was operating some type of motorized vehicle. If the charge is one of reckless homicide, if the offender is found to have been under the influence of drugs or alcohol at the time of the crime, this may serve as evidence of recklessness.

Both involuntary manslaughter and reckless homicide are Class 3 felonies. According to 730 ILCS 5/5-8-1(6), the sentence of imprisonment for a Class 3 felony shall be a minimum of 3 years and a maximum of 7 years. However, under certain circumstances outlined in the statute, the crimes may be upgraded to Class 2 felonies punishable by a term of imprisonment of not less than 3 years and not more than 14 years. In addition, if the defendant was under the influence of alcohol or drugs and killed more than one victim during the offense, the term of imprisonment shall be not less than 6 years and not more than 28 years.

FORCIBLE RAPE/CRIMINAL SEXUAL ASSAULT

In the Uniform Crime Reporting Program, **forcible rape** is defined as "the carnal knowledge of a female forcibly and against her will." Schmalleger discusses the crime of forcible rape on pp.42-45. In Florida, the crime of rape has been replaced with that of **criminal sexual assault**, which is discussed in 720 ILCS 5/12-12 through 12/18. This is a gender-neutral crime and does not specify the gender of the offender or the victim. Therefore, in Illinois, either a male or female offender may be convicted of the criminal sexual assault of either a male or female victim.

Criminal sexual assault is defined in 720 ILCS 5/12-13, which states that:

> (a) The accused commits criminal sexual assault if he or she:
> (1) commits an act of sexual penetration by the use of force or threat of force; or
> (2) commits an act of sexual penetration and the accused knew that the victim was unable to understand the nature of the act or was unable to give knowing consent; or

(3) commits an act of sexual penetration with a victim who was under 18 years of age when the act was committed and the accused was a family member; or

(4) commits an act of sexual penetration with a victim who was at least 13 years of age but under 18 years of age when the act was committed and the accused was 17 years of age or over and held a position of trust, authority or supervision in relation to the victim.

Sexual penetration is defined in 720 ILCS 5/12-12(f) and is limited to penetration by body parts, rather than other objects.

Criminal sexual assault is a Class 1 felony, which is punishable by a sentence of imprisonment of not less than 4 years and not more than 15 years.

Illinois also recognizes the crime of **aggravated criminal sexual assault**, which is a more serious crime. Effectively, this crime is criminal sexual assault with the presence of one of a number of specific aggravating factors. This crime is defined in 720 ILCS 5/12-14, which states that:

(a) The accused commits aggravated criminal sexual assault if he or she commits criminal sexual assault and any of the following aggravating circumstances existed during, or for the purposes of paragraph (7) of this subsection (a) as part of the same course of conduct as, the commission of the offense:

(1) the accused displayed, threatened to use, or used a dangerous weapon, other than a firearm, or any object fashioned or utilized in such a manner as to lead the victim under the circumstances reasonably to believe it to be a dangerous weapon; or

(2) the accused caused bodily harm, except as provided in subsection (a)(10), to the victim; or

(3) the accused acted in such a manner as to threaten or endanger the life of the victim or any other person; or

(4) the criminal sexual assault was perpetrated during the course of the commission or attempted commission of any other felony by the accused; or

(5) the victim was 60 years of age or over when the offense was committed; or

(6) the victim was a physically handicapped person; or

(7) the accused delivered (by injection, inhalation, ingestion, transfer of possession, or any other means) to the victim without his or her consent, or by threat or deception, and for other than medical purposes, any controlled substance; or

(8) the accused was armed with a firearm; or

(9) the accused personally discharged a firearm during the commission of the offense; or

(10) the accused, during the commission of the offense, personally discharged a firearm that proximately caused great bodily harm,

permanent disability, permanent disfigurement, or death to another person.
(b) The accused commits aggravated criminal sexual assault if the accused was under 17 years of age and (i) commits an act of sexual penetration with a victim who was under 9 years of age when the act was committed; or (ii) commits an act of sexual penetration with a victim who was at least 9 years of age but under 13 years of age when the act was committed and the accused used force or threat of force to commit the act.
(c) The accused commits aggravated criminal sexual assault if he or she commits an act of sexual penetration with a victim who was an institutionalized severely or profoundly mentally retarded person at the time the act was committed.

Aggravated criminal sexual assault is a Class X felony, which is punishable by a term of imprisonment of not less than 6 years nor more than 30 years. However, if the accused was armed with a firearm at the time of the crime, 15 years will be added to the term of imprisonment that the court imposes. If the accused discharged the firearm during the commission of the offense, 20 years will be added to the term of imprisonment. If the accused discharged a firearm and injured or killed another person, 25 years or up to a term of natural life imprisonment will be added to the term imposed by the court.

If the crime requires the element of the use of force or threat of force, the defendant may use as a defense that the victim consented to the act. 720 ILCS 5/12-17 defines consent as:

> "Consent" means a freely given agreement to the act of sexual penetration or sexual conduct in question. Lack of verbal or physical resistance or submission by the victim resulting from the use of force or threat of force by the accused shall not constitute consent. The manner of dress of the victim at the time of the offense shall not constitute consent.

Note that, in Illinois, it is not necessary for the victim to resist physically for the act to be a crime.

ROBBERY

Schmalleger discusses the crime of **robbery** on p.45. In Illinois, 720 ILCS 5/18-1 states that:

(a) A person commits robbery when he or she takes property, except a motor vehicle ... from the person or presence of another by the use of force or by threatening the imminent use of force.

This definition presents robbery as a theft in which the property is taken from the immediate presence or control of the victim and against the victim's will, using either force or the threat of force. This element of force is what distinguishes robbery from theft. Because of the use of force or fear to illegally acquire personal property, Illinois considers robbery to be both a crime against the person and a crime against property.

Actual force or violence is not required in the crime of robbery; it is sufficient to threaten the victim with force. Thus, either force or threat of force is sufficient to meet the requirement outlined in the definition of robbery. The victim is not required by law to have resisted physically in any way. The statute does not define the means by which the force is used or fear is imposed

Because the element of theft is a requirement for the crime of robbery, if no property is actually taken, the defendant cannot be found guilty of robbery.

Robbery in Illinois is a Class 2 felony, which generally is punishable by a sentence of imprisonment for at least 3 years but no more than 7 years. However, the statute states that the crime becomes a Class 1 felony in the following circumstances:

- the victim was at least 60 years of age
- the victim was physically handicapped
- the crime took place in a school or a place of worship

A Class 1 felony is punishable by a term of imprisonment of not less than 4 years nor more than 15 years.

Aggravated robbery is discussed in 720 ILCS 5/18-5. This statute states that:

> (a) A person commits aggravated robbery when he or she takes property from the person or presence of another by the use of force or by threatening the imminent use of force while indicating verbally or by his or her actions to the victim that he or she is presently armed with a firearm or other dangerous weapon, including a knife, club, ax, or bludgeon. This offense shall be applicable even though it is later determined that he or she had no firearm or other dangerous weapon, including a knife, club, ax, or bludgeon, in his or her possession when he or she committed the robbery.
>
> (a-5) A person commits aggravated robbery when he or she takes property from the person or presence of another by delivering ... to the victim without his or her consent, or by threat or deception, and for other than medical purposes, any controlled substance.

This crime, which is considered to be more serious than simple robbery, is a Class 1 felony, which is punishable by a term of imprisonment of not less than 4 years and not more than 15 years.

The most serious type of robbery in Illinois is the crime of **armed robbery**. Armed robbery is discussed in 720 ILCS 5/18-2, which states that:

(a) A person commits armed robbery when he or she violates Section 18-1; and
   (1) he or she carries on or about his or her person or is otherwise armed with a dangerous weapon other than a firearm; or
   (2) he or she carries on or about his or her person or is otherwise armed with a firearm; or
   (3) he or she, during the commission of the offense, personally discharges a firearm; or
   (4) he or she, during the commission of the offense, personally discharges a firearm that proximately causes great bodily harm, permanent disability, permanent disfigurement, or death to another person.

Armed robbery is classified as a Class X felony which is generally punishable by a term of incarceration of at least 6 years but not more than 30 years. However, the actual sentence depends upon which section of the statute was violated by the offender; violations of sections 2, 3, and 4 of this statute carry additional terms of imprisonment which are added on to the term imposed by the court.

The crime of **carjacking**, or **vehicular hijacking** as it is called in Illinois, is a separate category of robbery (see Schmalleger, p.50 for a discussion of carjacking). Vehicular hijacking, which is a Class 1 felony, is defined in 720 ILCS 5/18-3:

(a) A person commits vehicular hijacking when he or she takes a motor vehicle from the person or the immediate presence of another by the use of force or by threatening the imminent use of force.

The crime becomes **aggravated vehicular hijacking**, as defined in 720 ILCS 5/18-4, if it is committed in one of the following circumstances:

- the victim is at least 60 years of age or is physically handicapped
- there is a passenger in the vehicle who is under 16 years of age
- the offender is armed with a dangerous weapon other than a firearm
- the offender is armed with a firearm
- the offender discharges a firearm during the commission of the offense
- the offender discharges a firearm that causes great bodily harm or death to another person.

Aggravated vehicular hijacking is a Class X felony. However, depending on which section of the statute is violated, additional years may be added to the term of imprisonment imposed by the court.

Essentially, carjacking is the robbery of a motor vehicle. The victim does not need to be the owner of the vehicle, only to have custody of the vehicle at the time of the crime. The requirements regarding force and fear are the same as for robbery.

ASSAULT AND BATTERY

There is often some confusion about the actual meaning of **assault**. Although many people believe that assault involves inflicting an injury upon another person, in reality this is not the case: an assault is an intentional attempt or threat to cause injury. If the injury is actually inflicted, a **battery** has occurred. Effectively, an assault is an attempted battery. Therefore, there is no such crime as an attempted assault in Illinois.

The Uniform Crime Reporting Program focuses specifically on **aggravated assault**, which it defines as:

> an unlawful attack by one person upon another for the purpose of inflicting severe or aggravated bodily injury. This type of assault is usually accompanied by the use of a weapon or by means likely to produce death or great bodily harm.

Schmalleger discusses the crimes of simple and aggravated assault on p.48. In Illinois, assault is defined in 720 ILCS 5/12-1, which states that:

> (a) A person commits an assault when, without lawful authority, he engages in conduct which places another in reasonable apprehension of receiving a battery.

Simple assault is a Class C misdemeanor in Illinois. The statute states that, in addition to any other non-incarcerative punishment imposed by the court, the offender shall also be ordered to perform at least 30 and not more than 120 hours of community service. However, if the offender is sentenced to a term of incarceration, the requirement to perform community service does not apply.

Aggravated assault, which is discussed in 720 ILCS 5/12-2, is effectively an assault committed with aggravating circumstances, such as assault committed against a school employee on the grounds of a school, assault committed against a police officer, emergency medical technician, or firefighter, assault committed against a victim who is at least 60 years of age or who is physically handicapped, or assault involving the discharge of a firearm. Aggravated assault may be either a misdemeanor or a felony, depending on the circumstances of the crime.

The crime of **battery**, which is a Class A misdemeanor in Illinois, is defined in 720 ILCS 5/12-3:

> (a) A person commits battery if he intentionally or knowingly without legal justification and by any means, (1) causes bodily harm to an individual or (2) makes physical contact of an insulting or provoking nature with an individual.

The crime becomes **aggravated battery**, a Class 3 felony, if there are aggravating circumstances, such as battery that causes great bodily harm to the victim, battery using a deadly weapon other than a firearm, battery when the offender is hooded or masked, etc. The full list of aggravating circumstances is found in 720 ILCS 5/12-4, which defines the crime. If the offender causes great bodily harm to the victim through the use of some type of caustic or flammable substance, chemical contaminant, or bomb, the crime is one of **henious battery**, which is defined in 720 ILCS 5/12-4.1 as a Class X felony which is punishable by a term of imprisonment of not less than 6 years nor more than 45 years.

Illinois recognizes several other categories of battery. These include:

- domestic battery - 720 ILCS 5/12-3.2
- aggravated domestic battery - 720 ILCS 5/12-3.3
- aggravated battery with a firearm - 720 ILCS 5/12-4.2
- aggravated battery with a machine gun or a firearm equipped with any device or attachment designed or used for silencing the report of a firearm - 720 ILCS 5/12-4.2-5
- aggravated battery of a child - 720 ILCS 5/12-4.3
- aggravated battery of an unborn child - 720 ILCS 5/12-4.4
- aggravated battery of a senior citizen - 720 ILCS 5/12-4.6

BURGLARY

In common law, the crime of **burglary** was defined as the breaking and entering of a dwelling at night with intent to commit a felony. Today, the definition of burglary includes structures other than a dwelling place, can occur during the daytime as well as at night, and can involve either an intended felony or misdemeanor. Schmalleger discusses burglary on pp.48-49. The UCR defines burglary as the "unlawful entry of a structure to commit a felony or theft."

Burglary is defined in 720 ILCS 5/19-1, which states that:

> (a) A person commits burglary when without authority he knowingly enters or without authority remains within a building, housetrailer, watercraft, aircraft, motor vehicle as defined in The Illinois Vehicle Code, railroad car, or any part thereof, with intent to commit therein a felony or theft. This offense shall not include the offenses set out in Section 4-102 of The Illinois Vehicle Code, nor the offense of residential burglary as defined in Section 19-3 hereof.

Burglary is generally a Class 2 felony, unless it is committed in a school or a place of worship, when it is increased to a Class 1 felony.

If the property being burglarized is a residence, then the crime becomes one of **residential burglary**, which is defined in 720 ILCS 5/19-3 as:

(a) A person commits residential burglary who knowingly and without authority enters the dwelling place of another with the intent to commit therein a felony or theft.

Residential burglary is a Class 1 felony; it is considered to be more serious than a simple burglary. Essentially, burglary has two key elements:

1. The offender must unlawfully enter or remain within one of the locations defined by statute

2. The offender must have the intent to commit a felony or theft within this location

Because the second element only includes intent, the crime of burglary is completed when the offender enters the building, regardless of whether the offense intended to be committed within the structure was actually carried out. While the crime requires entry, forcible entry or "breaking" is not required in Illinois; any form of entry with intent is enough to constitute the crime of burglary. A burglary may even occur if the owner of the building invited the offender into the building or in some other way gave the offender permission to enter; if the offender enters with authority but remains without authority, the element is satisfied. Therefore, if an individual enters the location at a time when it was open to the public (e.g., entering a shop during regular business hours) but remains within after he/she knew that the premises were closed to the public, he/she may be guilty of burglary. In addition, if the offender is an a location that is open to the public but enters or remains in areas of the location that he/she knew or should have known were not open to the public, he/she may be guilty of burglary. However, an individual cannot be found guilty of burglarizing his or her own property as he/she has the legal right to enter and remain on the premises. Nor can an individual be found guilty of residential burglary if the property is his or her own residence.

LARCENY-THEFT

The FBI defines **larceny-theft** as:

the unlawful taking, carrying, leading, or riding away of property from the possession or constructive possession of another. It includes crimes such as shoplifting, pocket-picking, purse-snatching, thefts from motor vehicles, thefts of motor vehicle parts and accessories, bicycle thefts, etc., in which no use of force, violence, or fraud occurs.

Schmalleger discusses the crime of larceny on pp.49-50. In Illinois, the equivalent crime is known simply as **theft**. 720 ILCS 5/16-1 states that:

(a) A person commits theft when he knowingly:
(1) Obtains or exerts unauthorized control over property of the owner; or

(2) Obtains by deception control over property of the owner; or
(3) Obtains by threat control over property of the owner; or
(4) Obtains control over stolen property knowing the property to have been stolen or under such circumstances as would reasonably induce him to believe that the property was stolen; or
(5) Obtains or exerts control over property in the custody of any law enforcement agency which is explicitly represented to him by any law enforcement officer or any individual acting in behalf of a law enforcement agency as being stolen, and
   (A) Intends to deprive the owner permanently of the use or benefit of the property; or
   (B) Knowingly uses, conceals or abandons the property in such manner as to deprive the owner permanently of such use or benefit; or
   (C) Uses, conceals, or abandons the property knowing such use, concealment or abandonment probably will deprive the owner permanently of such use or benefit.

Even if the personal property stolen is something that is unlawful to possess (e.g., illegal drugs), the offender could still be convicted of the crime of theft.

According to 720 ILCS 5/15-1, **property** is defined as anything of value, including:

> real estate, money, commercial instruments, admission or transportation tickets, written instruments representing or embodying rights concerning anything of value, labor, or services, or otherwise of value to the owner; things growing on, affixed to, or found on land, or part of or affixed to any building; electricity, gas and water; telecommunications services; birds, animals and fish, which ordinarily are kept in a state of confinement; food and drink; samples, cultures, microorganisms, specimens, records, recordings, documents, blueprints, drawings, maps, and whole or partial copies, descriptions, photographs, computer programs or data, prototypes or models thereof, or any other articles, materials, devices, substances and whole or partial copies, descriptions, photographs, prototypes, or models thereof which constitute, represent, evidence, reflect or record a secret scientific, technical, merchandising, production or management information, design, process, procedure, formula, invention, or improvement.

The **owner** of the property is defined in 720 ILCS 5/15-2 as:

> a person, other than the offender, who has possession of or any other interest in the property involved, even though such interest or possession is unlawful, and without whose consent the offender has no authority to exert control over the property.

720 ILCS 5/16-4 discusses the possible situation of the offender having some interest in the property that he/she stole. However, the statute states that this is not a defense against a charge of theft of property if the owner also has an interest in the property to which the offender is not entitled. The

statute also discusses the issue of theft by a spouse. If the property is owned by the offender's spouse, the crime of theft may only be prosecuted if the two parties were not living together as spouses and were living in separate dwellings at the time of the crime.

The level of seriousness of the crime depends on the circumstances surrounding the offense. The possible classifications of the crime of theft are outlined in 720 5/16-1, which states that:

> (b) Sentence.
> (1) Theft of property, other than a firearm, not from the person and not exceeding $300 in value is a Class A misdemeanor.
> (2) A person who has been convicted of theft of property not exceeding $300 in value, other than a firearm and not from the person, who has been previously convicted of any type of theft, robbery, armed robbery, burglary, residential burglary, possession of burglary tools, home invasion, forgery, a violation of Section 4-103, 4-103.1, 4-103.2, or 4-103.3 of the Illinois Vehicle Code relating to the possession of a stolen or converted motor vehicle, or a violation of Section 8 of the Illinois Credit Card and Debit Card Act is guilty of a Class 4 felony...
> (3) Theft of a firearm not from the person regardless of value is a Class 4 felony. A second or subsequent such offense is a Class 3 felony.
> (4) Theft of property from the person not exceeding $300 in value, or theft of property exceeding $300 and not exceeding $10,000 in value, is a Class 3 felony.
> (5) Theft of property exceeding $10,000 and not exceeding $100,000 in value is a Class 2 felony.
> (6) Theft of property exceeding $100,000 in value is a Class 1 felony.
> (7) Theft by deception, as described by paragraph (2) of subsection (a) of this Section, in which the offender obtained money or property valued at $5,000 or more from a victim 60 years of age or older is a Class 2 felony.

Clearly, the classification depends primarily on the actual value of the property that was stolen. 720 ILCS 5/15-9 discusses how the value of property is determined. According to the statute:

> the "value" of property consisting of any commercial instrument or any written instrument representing or embodying rights concerning anything of value, labor, or services or otherwise of value to the owner shall be:
> (a) The "market value" of such instrument if such instrument is negotiable and has a market value; and
> (b) The "actual value" of such instrument if such instrument is not negotiable or is otherwise without a market value. For the purpose of establishing such "actual value", the interest of any owner or owners entitled to part or all of the property represented by such instrument, by reason of such

instrument, may be shown, even if another "owner" may be
named in the complaint, information or indictment.

MOTOR VEHICLE THEFT

The UCR considers **motor vehicle theft** to be a separate index crime from that of theft or larceny-theft. Schmalleger discusses this crime on p.50. It is defined by the FBI as:

> the theft or attempted theft of a motor vehicle, this offense category includes the stealing of automobiles, trucks, buses, motorcycles, motorscooters, snowmobiles, etc.

While Illinois does not consider motor vehicle theft to be a separate crime, there are several crimes outlined in the Florida Statutes which correspond to this index crime. The statutory definition of theft (720 ICLS 5/16-1) includes the theft of a motor vehicle. However, it is necessary to prove that the offender indented to permanently deprive the owner of the property to convict an offender under this statute and it may be difficult to prove such intent.

Carjacking, or vehicular hijacking is defined in 720 ILCS 5/18-3 and aggravated vehicular hijacking is defined in 720 ILCS 5/18-4 (see the discussion under **Robbery** earlier in this chapter). These crimes do involve the taking of a motor vehicle from another's person or custody. While the UCR considers carjacking to be a form of motor vehicle theft, it involves the use of force or threat of force and are considered in Illinois to be forms of robbery rather than theft.

ARSON

Like burglary, the common-law felony crime of **arson** was a crime against a home or dwelling place. While it could occur at any time of day, nighttime arson was considered to be a more serious crime. Schmalleger discusses the crime of arson on p.51. The UCR defines arson as:

> any willful or malicious burning or attempt to burn, with or without intent to defraud, a dwelling house, public building, motor vehicle or aircraft, personal property of another, etc.

Today, Illinois law recognizes arson against structures other than a home as well as the burning of other types of property. There are several categories of arson outlined in the Illinois Criminal Code: **arson**, **residential arson**, and **aggravated arson**.

Simple arson, a Class 2 felony, is defined in 720 ILCS 5/20-1, which states that:

> A person commits arson when, by means of fire or explosive, he knowingly:
> (a) Damages any real property, or any personal property having a value of $150 or more, of another without his consent; or

> (b) With intent to defraud an insurer, damages any property or any personal property having a value of $150 or more.
>
> Property "of another" means a building or other property, whether real or personal, in which a person other than the offender has an interest which the offender has no authority to defeat or impair, even though the offender may also have an interest in the building or property.

Because of the type of location victimized, residential arson is considered to be more serious than simple arson. It is a Class 1 felony. According to 720 ILCS 5/20-1.2,

> (a) A person commits the offense of residential arson when, in the course of committing an arson, he or she knowingly damages, partially or totally, any building or structure that is the dwelling place of another.

Finally, the most serious form of arson, aggravated arson, is a Class X felony. It is considered to be a more henious crime because of the increased possibility that persons may be present in the structure and/or injured as a result of the fire. Aggravated arson is defined in 720 ILCS 5/20-1.1 as:

> (a) A person commits aggravated arson when in the course of committing arson he knowingly damages, partially or totally, any building or structure, including any adjacent building or structure, and (1) he knows or reasonably should know that one or more persons are present therein or (2) any person suffers great bodily harm, or permanent disability or disfigurement as a result of the fire or explosion or (3) a fireman or policeman who is present at the scene acting in the line of duty, is injured as a result of the fire or explosion.

Intent is required for arson; a fire that is of accidently or unintentional origin is not considered to be arson. If a person burns his or her own personal property, it may still be arson if the damaged property was an occupied structure or if the offender intended to defraud an insurer. However, the statute defining residential arson does specify that the location burned is the residence of another person.

HATE CRIMES

Schmalleger (pp.53-56) discusses the issue of **hate crimes**. He defines a hate crime as:

> A criminal offense in which the motive was hatred, bias, or prejudice, based on the actual or perceived race, color, religion, national origin, ethnicity, gender, or sexual orientation of another individual or group of individuals.

While hate crimes are not specifically included in the UCR's eight index crimes, the FBI began to collect data on this category of crime after President Bush signed the Hate Crimes Statistics Act in 1990.

720 ILCS 5/12-7.1 specifically discusses hate crimes. Hate crimes are defined in Illinois as:

> (a) A person commits hate crime when, by reason of the actual or perceived race, color, creed, religion, ancestry, gender, sexual orientation, physical or mental disability, or national origin of another individual or group of individuals, he commits assault, battery, aggravated assault, misdemeanor theft, criminal trespass to residence, misdemeanor criminal damage to property, criminal trespass to vehicle, criminal trespass to real property, mob action or disorderly conduct ... or harassment by telephone ... against a victim who is:
> (i) the other individual;
> (ii) a member of the group of individuals;
> (iii) a person who has an association with, is married to, or has a friendship with the other individual or a member of the group of individuals; or
> (iv) a relative (by blood or marriage) of a person described in clause (i), (ii), or (iii).

According to the statute, sexual orientation includes heterosexuality, homosexuality, or bisexuality. The first offense under this statute is considered to be a Class 4 felony; subsequent offenses are Class 2 felonies.

In 1999, the Governor's Commission on Discrimination and Hate Crimes was established by Governor George H. Ryan. The Commission, which has 40 members, works with the criminal justice system as well as social service agencies, community organizations, schools, and religious groups to prevent hate crimes and discrimination and to increase acceptance and tolerance.

CHAPTER 4

THE POLICE IN ILLINOIS

INTRODUCTION

Schmalleger (see Chapter 5) discusses the topic of the various levels of law enforcement in the United States today. It is clear that there are many levels of police agencies in America: federal law enforcement, state police, county sheriff's agencies, and city police.

There are over 1,100 separate law enforcement agencies in Illinois today. Over 900 local or municipal departments; in addition, there are 102 county sheriff's departments, one state police agency (the Illinois State Police), and a wide variety of special-purpose law enforcement agencies at all levels of government. In 1998, there were 38,569 full- and part-time sworn officers employed in the various law enforcement agencies in the state. This made up approximately 76 percent of the law enforcement community's workforce in the state. In addition, there were 9,667 civilian employees and 2,614 auxiliary officers. Of the total number of sworn officers employed in Illinois, 29,528 worked in municipal departments, 4,077 in sheriff's offices, and, 4,964 in the other miscellaneous agencies throughout the state.

Illinois has a number of special law enforcement problems, including issues such as drugs, immigration, and tourism. Because of this, a large number of federal law enforcement agencies have offices in Illinois and/or are involved in law enforcement activities within the state. This includes the Federal Bureau of Investigation, the Drug Enforcement Agency, and the Bureau of Alcohol, Tobacco, and Firearms. This results in a considerable amount of overlap among the various levels of law enforcement in the state. See Schmalleger (pp.177-180) for a discussion of some of the key federal law enforcement agencies in the United States.

LOCAL POLICING

Schmalleger (see p.183) briefly discusses the topic of local policing in the United States. The majority of the police departments in Florida are local or city departments. Currently, there are almost 700 separate local police agencies in the state. Every local department is independent of every other department. The goals, purposes, and priorities vary greatly among departments, with each local agency responding to the needs and desires of the population it serves. All municipal police departments are full-service police agencies which provide a wide range of police services, including law enforcement, order maintenance, and service.

In 1998, there were a total of 29,528 sworn officers employed in local police departments in Illinois, which accounted for approximately 80 percent of the police department work force. The employment rate for sworn employees of local departments in 1998 was 3.0 per 1,000 inhabitants. In addition, there were 5,574 civilian employees, making up approximately 15 percent of the work force, with an employment rate of 0.6 per 1,000 inhabitants, and 1,710 auxiliary officers, making up almost 5 percent of the work force, with an employment rate of 0.2 per 1,000 inhabitants.

The largest local police department in Illinois is the Chicago Police Department, with over 16,500 employees. This includes approximately 13,500 sworn officers, over 2,000 civilian employees, and 1,000 crossing guards. In contrast, there are a number of local departments with no more than five sworn officers and several with only one sworn officer.

The Chicago Police Department

The City of Chicago, located in Cook County, received its city charter in 1837. Today it has a population of almost 3 million people. The largest city agency in Chicago is the **Chicago Police Department** (CPD). The CPD is organized into five bureaus. The largest is the **Bureau of Operational Services**, which employs the majority of the department's officers. The Bureau includes not only the Patrol Division but also a number of special functions (e.g., public housing, traffic, airport law enforcement, and public transportation). The **Bureau of Investigative Services** conducts follow-up investigations of crimes and apprehends offenders and is also involved in investigating narcotics, gang crime, auto theft, arson, vice, and various juvenile matters. The Detective Division is housed in this Bureau along with the Organized Crime and Youth Divisions. Departmental technical and support functions are carried out by the **Bureau of Technical Services**. The Bureau's duties include processing evidence and recovered property, maintaining departmental equipment and vehicles, running the auto impound, and the detention and transportation of arrested individuals. The **Bureau of Staff Services** is responsible for the CPD's education and training programs, management and labor affairs, and centralized crime prevention, as well as various internal control functions. It also provides professional counseling to CPD members. Finally, the **Bureau of Administrative Services** is responsible for the department's basic administrative functions, such as data systems, personnel, finance, and records.

In April 1993, the CPD implemented a new community policing philosophy known as the **Chicago Alternative Policing Strategy** (CAPS). The program was tested in five of the city's 25 police districts before being implemented city-wide in 1994. CAPS emphasizes problem-identification and problem-solving at the neighborhood level, and includes the use of neighborhood-based beat officers, regularly-scheduled Beat Community Meetings that involve both residents and police, and the use of new technology to target "hot spots" of crime.

CAPS emphasizes the need for a partnership between the police, other Chicago government agencies, and the community. There are a number of key components to this partnership. One is the use of **beat officers**. The program assigns eight or nine beat patrol officers to each of the 279 beats in Chicago. These officers remain on the same beat and on the same watch for at least a year, allowing them to interact with and get to know the neighborhood and giving members of the community an opportunity to get to know their beat officers. Beat officers patrol primarily in cars but occasionally patrol on foot. The program emphasizes beat integrity, which allows officers to remain on their assigned beats and address problems specific to their neighborhood. Beat officers not only answer calls for service but also work to proactively solve crime and disorder problems on the beat.

In addition, each district has teams of **rapid response officers** who support the work of the beat officers, respond to many of the emergency calls for service to allow the beat officers to remain on their assigned beats, and provide backup for beat officers when they are working with the community or attending community beat meetings. In addition, plainclothes gang and tactical officers are assigned to each district; their focus on solving crimes and apprehending offenders also supports the work of the beat officers.

Another element of CAPS is **Beat Community Meetings**. There are 279 police beats in the city; each one holds regular community meetings, usually monthly or bi-monthly. These meetings, which are hosted by the CPD, bring together beat patrol officers and neighborhood residents in a positive environment which allows them to work together to identify, analyze and begin to solve crime problems in the neighborhood. Residents and police exchange information about neighborhood conditions, identify problems of crime and disorder, and develop strategies to deal with these problems, as well as allowing the police and members of the community to meet and get to know each another.

Neighborhood problem solving is another key component of CAPS. Officers receive training in how to solve neighborhood problems of crime and disorder instead of reacting to immediate symptoms. They use a five-step problem-solving process. The first step is to **identify and prioritize** the problem. The problem is then **analyzed** from the multiple perspectives of offenders, victims, and location to better understand the issues underlying the problem. The third step is to **design strategies** to deal with the problem. Frequently, multiple strategies may be developed, each focusing on a different perspective of the problem. Next, the strategies are **implemented** or put into place. Finally, the entire procedure is **evaluated** to determine if the various strategies worked. Strategies that do not appear to be successful may be stopped or altered.

Other important elements of CAPS include the use of new technology, needed support from other city agencies, a Court Advocacy Program, and CAPS training for both police and members of the community.

Minimum qualifications that applicants to the CPD must meet include:

- minimum age of 22
- have a valid driver's license
- have at least 60 semester or 90 quarter credit hours from an accredited college or university
- must be a resident in the city of Chicago

Qualified individuals first go through a written examination which eliminates the majority of applicants. Those who qualify for participation in the next stages of the hiring process must pass a background investigation, a psychological examination, medical tests, drug screening, and physical fitness tests. Base salaries in 2000 started at $33,522.

The Peoria Police Department

Peoria is the second-largest metropolis in the state of Illinois. It was incorporated as a village in 1835, the same year the first city jail was constructed. At this time, law enforcement was the responsibility of the town marshal. However, in 1837 the first chief of police was appointed. In 1845, Peoria was incorporated as a city and the first mayor was elected. By 1863 the **Peoria Police Department** (PPD) had 16 officers, all of whom were appointed by the mayor. The system of mayoral appointment meant that each time a new mayor was elected, he/she could appoint and/or remove anyone in the entire department. However, in most cases, the new mayor would only remove command officers.

By 1884, the department had grown to 40 officers. In 1886, the first patrol box was introduced, allowing beat patrol officers to check in regularly with headquarters. The first police matron, Albina Banett, was hired in 1890 and given the duties of handling female prisoners and working with children. The first black police officer was hired in 1903. In the same year the first PPD officer was killed in the line of duty.

In 1906, the PPD had a total of 67 employees. Annual salaries in 1906 were $600 for patrol officers, $900 for the one lieutenant in the department, $1,200 for the one captain, and $1,500 for the Superintendent of Police. Patrol officers at this time were assigned to twelve-hour shifts. They worked seven days a week with one day off per month. In 1910, the city of Peoria adopted the Civil Service Act, which placed the police department under civil service. This removed from the mayor the power of appointing police officers.

In 1934, the PPD became one of the first police departments in the United States to use two-way police radios. The main station was equipped with a radio and additional units were placed in each patrol car. During the same year, the department's Accident Investigation Squad was created to handle all accidents and the department's record system was created. In 1935, the first policewoman was hired, although she made less than the department matrons. By 1938, the PPD had a total of 135 commissioned personnel, including two policewomen and two matrons. There was a clear salary differential for male and female officers; a second class patrolman made $1,560 per year while policewomen and matrons received an annual salary of $960. This disparity would continue; in 1953 a second third-class patrolman received $3,680 per year while policewomen and matrons received $3,360 per year.

The department began formal in-service training for rookie officers in 1939; the training lasted a total of two weeks. In 1957, the PPD became the first department in Illinois to use police dogs. The Police-Community Relations Program was first developed in 1967; that same year, William Helm became the first African American in the PPD to be promoted to the rank of Captain. In 1969, Mary Dunlavey became the first woman to reach the rank of Sergeant in the PPD.

In the 1990s, the PPD focused heavily on the development of community policing programs and the concept of building a partnership with the community. A gang unit was formed in 1996; it was merged with the Community Area Target Team in 1999 to form the new Street Crime Unit.

The department is divided into several service areas. **Uniform Services** includes the department's Patrol Division, which has approximately 250 sworn personnel. The responsibilities of the Patrol Division include apprehending offenders, protecting life and property, and maintaining order. Officers issue traffic citations, provide traffic control, and investigate traffic accidents. The Patrol Division includes the department's Street Crime Unit, K-9 Unit, and a special PHA Walking Beat program which is a cooperative venture between the PPD and the Peoria Housing Authority.

The **Criminal Investigations Division** identifies and apprehends offenders and prepares cases for prosecution. The Juvenile Unit is located within this Division; it works to develop and implement programs to prevent and control juvenile crime and delinquency. The Division's Special Investigations Unit focuses specifically on vice and narcotics. The **Support Services Division** provides a variety of support functions for the department. The Division maintains departmental records, such as criminal histories and arrest records. It also ensures the security and property disposition of seized property and physical evidence, as well as supervising the PPD Crime Lab.

Minimum requirements for application to the PPD include:

- minimum age of 21 by the date of the written exam (or a minimum age of 20 for applicants who have completed 60 semester hours of law enforcement studies at an accredited college or university)
- maximum age of 35 by date of entrance into the eligibility pool (exceptions are made for applicants with prior municipal police experience)
- high school diploma or GED equivalent (the department prefers applicants who have an associate's degree or credit hours toward a degree)
- U.S citizen
- have a valid driver's license
- must be in adequate physical condition to perform the functions of the job and to pass a physical agility exam
- no felony convictions
- uncorrected vision not less than 20/200 in either eye

Individuals meeting the minimum qualifications go through a series of written, oral and physical tests. Those who pass all these tests are placed in an eligibility pool for a two-year period and are considered for hire by the PPD as openings become available. If a candidate is offered employment, he/she must pass a background investigation, medical examination, polygraph test, and psychological evaluation. The minimum annual starting salary for recruits in 2000 was $32,818.34; this increases to $33,638.79 after academy training is completed. In 1999, the maximum pay for an officer was $49,694.45, not including various educational and longevity incentives.

COUNTY POLICING

Schmalleger covers the topic of county sheriff's departments in the United States in his discussion of local agencies (see p.183). Illinois has 102 counties, each with a separate sheriff's department and an elected sheriff. The office of sheriff is provided for in Article VII, Section 7c of the Illinois Constitution, which states that:

> Each county shall elect a sheriff, county clerk and treasurer and may elect or appoint a coroner, recorder, assessor, auditor and such other officers as provided by law or by county ordinance. Except as changed pursuant to this Section, elected county officers shall be elected for terms of four years at general elections as provided by law. Any office may be created or eliminated and the terms of office and manner of selection changed by county-wide referendum. Offices other than sheriff, county clerk and treasurer may be eliminated and the terms of office and manner of selection changed by law. Offices other than sheriff, county clerk, treasurer, coroner, recorder, assessor and auditor may be eliminated and the terms of office and manner of selection changed by county ordinance.

Sheriff's departments in Illinois are full-service police agencies providing police services to all unincorporated areas of the county. In addition, incorporated cities that do not wish to set up their own city police department may contract out to their county sheriff's department for police services. Sheriff's departments in Illinois are often responsible not only for providing law enforcement services to the county but also for running the county jail, maintaining security in all county courts, serving civil and criminal processes, and providing assistance when needed to local departments within the county. This assistance can range from operating a county-wide crime lab to assisting a local department with a criminal investigation.

In 1998, there were a total of 4,077 full- and part-time sworn officers employed in sheriff's departments in Illinois, which accounted for approximately 60 percent of the work force. The employment rate for sworn employees of sheriff's departments in 1998 was 1.8 per 1,000 inhabitants. In addition, there were 1,932 civilian employees, making up approximately 28 percent of the work force, with an employment rate of 0.9 per 1,000 inhabitants, and 825 auxiliary officers, making up 12 percent of the work force, with an employment rate of 0.4 per 1,000 inhabitants. The largest sheriff's office is the Cook County Sheriff's Police Department, with over 500 sworn officers; there are several departments with only five sworn officers.

The Lake County Sheriff's Office

The **Lake County Sheriff's Office** (LCSO) is the largest law enforcement agency in Lake county. The sheriff of Lake County, like all county sheriffs in Illinois, is elected by the county and serves terms of four years. The LCSO has a total of 171 sworn deputies and 229 civilian employees. The department's annual budget is approximately $24 million.

LCSO officers have the right to enforce the law throughout the county but generally the sheriff does not enforce the law within towns or municipalities that have their own police department, unless requested to do so by the community, or by federal or state authorities. In addition to law enforcement and crime prevention, the LCSO has a wide variety of responsibilities. These include serving civil documents (e.g., subpoenas, summonses, and judgements), dealing with property sales, foreclosures, and auctions, providing security for the Lake County Court Complex, and maintaining the Lake County Jail and the Lake County Work Release Center.

The LCSO has a number of divisions and programs. The **Highway Patrol Division** is responsible for patrolling the county's streets and highways and for responding to calls for service from the public. This is the basic uniformed division of the department: they keep the peace, arrest offenders, deal with traffic accidents and violations, and perform all the basic duties of a uniformed officer. It includes a deputy chief, twelve command officers, and 67 deputies. The division includes a K-9 unit, a tactical unit, an evidence technician unit, an accident investigation unit, a traffic enforcement unit, and a field training unit. In 1998, the Highway Patrol Division responded to a total of 268,347 calls for service as well as handling 5,487 traffic accidents.

The **Criminal Investigations Division** (CID) is responsible for the investigation of criminal activities throughout the county. The CID includes one deputy chief, three sergeants, and 16 investigators. There are two main units within this division. The general investigations unit focuses on all crimes committed by adult offenders. In 1998, investigators in this unit investigated a total of 1,797 criminal cases. They made a total of 799 arrests, of which 461 were felonies and 338 were misdemeanors. The juvenile investigation unit focuses on any situations involving juveniles, including not only juvenile offenders but also cases of missing children, runaways, and child abuse or neglect. In 1998, the unit investigated 956 cases as well as 330 incidents concerning missing or runaway children. In addition, the CID has deputies assigned several special units, including the Lake County Metropolitan Enforcement Group, which investigates drug activity in Lake County, the Lake County Children's Advocacy Center, which focuses on sexual or physical abuse of a juvenile by a caretaker, the Lake County Gang Task Force, the Lake County Major Crime Task Force, and the Lake County Repeat Offenders Strike Force.

The **Administration Division** includes the administrative staff of the LCSO. The division is responsible for both the daily administration of the department as well as long-term planning and organization. One key unit within this division is the internal affairs division (IAD), which is responsible for the investigation of any complaints related to members of the department. Complaints investigated include those involving allegations of false arrest, unnecessary use of force, excessive use of force, criminal violations, violations of department rules or policies, and discrimination.

The **Community Services and Crime Prevention Division** focuses on involving the community in crime prevention, through a variety of activities. The division provides written information to schools, community and civic groups, gives presentations on a variety of topics ranging from gang crime and substance abuse to home security and child safety. The division has focuses specifically on programs such as neighborhood watch and operation identification as ways of involving the public in crime prevention. The **Court Security Division** is responsible for providing security for the Lake County Court Complex. Deputies are assigned to each courtroom to protect the judge, guard the jury deliberation room, and generally maintain order within the courtroom.

The LCSO is also responsible for running the **Lake County Adult Correctional Facility**. This jail, which opened in 1989, can house a maximum of 602 detainees. The average daily population in 1998 was 543 detainees. The facility provides detainees with rehabilitative and educational programs, such as GED, ESOL, parenting courses, anger control, Alcoholics Anonymous, Narcotics Anonymous, substance abuse treatment, and various religious programs. The inmate work detail, which includes six to ten sentenced inmates of the jail, cleans road debris from county highways. The sheriff's office also runs the **Lake County Work Release Center**, which has space for a total of 110 residents;

during 1998, the average daily population was 110 inmates. Residents in this center are non-violent offenders who are allowed to continue maintaining employment while serving their sentences. They remain under correctional supervision when not at their place of employment and receive counseling and other rehabilitative programs. Inmates are required to pay room and board to the program; in 1998, the centered generated over $596,000 in room and board fees. Approximately 92 percent of residents complete the program with no violations.

The St. Clair County Sheriff's Department

The **St. Clair County Sheriff's Department** (SCCSD) is responsible for policing the unincorporated areas of St. Clair County, which is in Southern Illinois. The department has 128 full-time sworn deputies, 39 auxiliary deputies, and 20 civilian employees. In addition to providing a full range of policing services to the county, the department is also responsible for serving civil processes, providing court bailiffs, and providing correctional services to the county.

The **Patrol Division** of the department provides law enforcement services to the county, including police patrol, crime prevention, traffic services, and prisoner transport. The division includes an investigations unit, which houses the department's detectives. This unit focuses on the follow-up investigation of serious crimes (including all index crimes). The Pressure Point Unit is a special squad composed of three deputies who use aggressive proactive techniques in high-crime neighborhoods. Deputies in the patrol division also provide school resource officers and teach the D.A.R.E. program, as well as teaching crime prevention techniques to members of the community. In 1998, the patrol division responded to a total of 32,356 calls for service, answered 2,660 alarm calls, served over 10,000 warrants, and issued 6,668 traffic citations.

The **Civil Process Division** is responsible for serving a variety of civil documents, such as summons, judgments, and subpoenas. They also stand by during evictions. In 1998, the division, which employs three process servers as well as two full-time and one part-time clerk, served over 8,000 civil papers.

The **Correctional Division** is responsible for running the county jail. In 1998, over 10,00 inmates were admitted to the jail. Of these, approximately 83 percent were male. About 62 percent were black, 35 percent white, and 3 percent fell into other racial categories. The average length of stay was eleven days. The majority of the inmates (approximately 57 percent) were charged with misdemeanor offenses. The remainder were felons, fugitives held for another agency, offenders charged with federal crimes, or other categories of inmates. The department also runs a **Jail Work Release Program** in which detainees work out in the community mowing lawns, picking up trash, cleaning up dump sites, and washing police cars. Participants must be on non-escape and non-violent status and must volunteer to participate in the program.

The department has operated a Correctional Officers Training Academy since 1984, one year before Illinois mandated training for county correctional officers. The minimum standard training course is 200 hours long, and includes forty hours of firearms training as well as courses in criminal law, defense tactics, crisis intervention, and transportation of detainees.

STATE POLICING

Schmalleger (see pp.180-183) discusses **state police agencies** within the United States. Some states, such as Pennsylvania, operate a **centralized** or full-service state police agency which includes both highway patrol functions and criminal investigation. However, other states, such as North Carolina, separate or **decentralize** the functions and keep criminal investigations separate from the uniformed highway patrol. Illinois follows the centralized system; its main state law enforcement agency is the Illinois State Police.

The Illinois State Police

The **Illinois State Police** (ISP) was created in 1922, under the authorization of the Illinois General Assembly. Originally, the ISP's main purpose was to act as a highway patrol and enforce the provisions of the state's motor vehicle laws. The first officers patrolled the state highways on motorcycles. However, the agency has evolved into a full-service police department with the responsibility of enforcing not only the motor vehicle laws of the state but also the state's criminal laws, as well as providing a wide variety of services to the state. The ISP has over 3,000 employees, including both civilians and sworn officers. The agency has been accredited by the Commission on the Accreditation of Law Enforcement Agencies since 1986.

The ISP is divided into several key divisions, each providing specific services. The **Division of Operations** provides support to federal law enforcement agencies as well as to county and municipal police departments within the state. There are approximately 1700 officers employed in this division, which is involved in both criminal investigation and highway safety. Uniformed and plainclothes troopers assigned to this division patrol highways throughout the state. The division's Safety Education Officers give public presentations to schools, youth groups, and community groups on crime prevention, personal safety, and traffic safety. The division maintains K-9 units as well as underwater search and recovery teams and tactical response teams. These units assist other agencies throughout the state in a variety of investigations and emergencies. The division also has a dedicated fleet of aircraft which are used to spot illegally-grown drugs, help enforce traffic laws, search for missing persons, and recover fugitives. The ISP's **Division of Forensic Services** operates nine forensic sciences laboratories which are located throughout the state and which provide a variety of services to state, county, and local police officers, such as crime scene assistance, polygraph services, and a wide range of scientific tests. The division also maintains an Automated Fingerprint Identification System (AFIS), which links all the state labs and allows local departments to access the database.

The **Division of Internal Investigation** investigates allegations of corruption, misconduct, and malfeasance within any state governmental agency under the governor's jurisdiction. Issues examined by this division include charges of abuse or neglect of inmates housed in state mental or correctional facilities, financial crimes, and theft of state property. Finally, the **Division of Administration** provides administrative support to the department. For example, this division operates the state's Firearm Owner's Identification card program, to determine whether individuals applying to acquire, possess, or transfer firearms are eligible. The division also runs the department's Bureau of Identification, which holds all the criminal history records of the state. The division's Human Resource Command unit operates the Illinois State Police Academy, which provides basic training to ISP cadets. The Academy also provides in-service education to state troopers as well as local and county officers throughout the state.

In 1972, the ISP was given the responsibility of collecting state-wide crime statistics and reporting to the FBI's Uniform Crime Reports. 20 ILCS 2630/8 states that:

> The Department shall be a central repository and custodian of crime statistics for the State and it shall have all power incident thereto to carry out the purposes of this Act, including the power to demand and receive cooperation in the submission of crime statistics from all units of government...

The "Department" referred to in the statute is the ISP. All agencies participating in the Illinois Uniform Crime Reporting Program submit data on a monthly basis.

According to 20 ILCS 2610/9, the minimum requirements that must be met by applicants to the ISP include:

- minimum age of 21 (applicants who are 20 years old will be accepted if their education includes a law enforcement major)
- U.S. citizen
- valid driver's license
- no felony convictions
- willingness to accept assignments anywhere in the state of Illinois
- have a minimum of a "C" average in college classes
- must meet one of the following education requirements:
  - have a bachelor's degree
  - have an associate of arts or associates of science degree and at least three years continuous full-time service as a police officer with the same police agency
  - have an associate of applied science degree in law enforcement and at least three years continuous full-time service as a police officer with the same police agency
  - have 60 semester hours or 90 quarter hours of core subjects from an accredited college or university (including 9 semester hours in communication studies, 9 semester hours in social sciences, 9 semester hours in humanities, 6 semester hours in natural sciences, 3 semester hours in math, and 24 semester hours in any other electives)

Applicants go through a rigorous recruitment and selection process. The first step in the recruitment phase is the completion and submission of a **pre-employment inquiry card** (PIC). All requirements, including all college-level course-work, must be met before the applicant submits a PIC to the ISP's Merit Board. Applicants then participate in a mandatory **process orientation**, which explains the selection process and the physical ability test. After the orientation, applicants are invited to complete a four-item **Physical Ability Test** (PAT). The PAT includes a sit-and-reach test, a one-minute sit-up test, a one repetition maximum-bench press, and a 1.5 mile run. Applicants who successfully complete the PAT then complete a **background questionnaire** and are placed in the **eligibility pool**.

Applicants may remain in the eligibility pool for a period of one year, or until a cadet class is scheduled, whichever comes first.

After a cadet class is scheduled, applicants move into the selection phase. The first step is **suitability testing**, which includes a number of written tests. Applicants then go through a **polygraph test**. Those applicants who are selected to advance from this phase go through a complete **background investigation**. Applicants who pass through this phase successfully are scheduled for a one-hour **oral interview**. After this step, all applicants are rank ordered, the number of applicants needed to fill the cadet class are taken from the rank order list, and they then go through a **suitability interview** with a psychologist. The number of applicants needed to fill the class are **certified** to the director of the Merit Board. After certification, the ISP Personnel Bureau contacts prospective cadets and makes an offer of employment, conditional upon the satisfactory completion of medical and academic examinations. The prospective cadets then undergo a **medical examination** performed by a physician approved by the ISP and go through ISP-administered academic testing. Those candidates who successfully complete the entire process are given cadet status and scheduled for academy training.

ISP cadets go through a 25-week residential training program at the ISP academy in Springfield. The cadets take courses in a variety of subjects, including ethics, criminal law, traffic law, radio procedures, community policing, report writing, firearms, problem solving, domestic violence, crash investigation, controlled substances, CPR and first responder, gang activity, stress management, traffic direction, crowd control, and critical thinking. Failure in any course can result in dismissal from the program. Cadets who successfully complete the academy program become probationary troopers and go through field training, working with three separate field training officers during the program. After successfully completing the field training program, the trooper remains on probationary status until the one-year anniversary from the date of entry into the academy. At the end of this period, the probationer becomes a full ISP trooper.

According to 20 ILCS 2610/12.1, state police officers may not continue in service after reaching the age of 60.

The Illinois Criminal Justice Information Authority

The **Illinois Criminal Justice Information Authority** (ICJIA) was originally created in 1973 as the Criminal Justice Information Systems Division of the Illinois Law Enforcement Commission. The agency focused on the development of standards for information systems for state and local governments in Illinois. The Commission was abolished in 1982 and the ICJIA was created by the passage of the Illinois Criminal Justice Information Act (20 ILCS 3930). According to 20 ILCS 3939/2:

> The purpose of this Act is to coordinate the use of information in the criminal justice system; to promulgate effective criminal justice information policy; to encourage the improvement of criminal justice agency procedures and practices with respect to information; to provide new information technologies; to permit the evaluation of information practices and programs; to stimulate research and development of new methods and uses of criminal justice information for the improvement of the criminal

justice system and the reduction of crime; and to protect the integrity of criminal history record information, while protecting the citizen's right to privacy.

The ICJIA has a total of sixteen members. These include the Attorney General, the Director of the Illinois Department of Corrections, the Director of the Illinois Department of State Police, the Sheriff of Cook County, the State's Attorney of Cook County, the Superintendent of the Chicago Police Department, the Director of the Office of the State's Attorneys Appellate Prosecutor, and the Executive Director of the Law Enforcement Training and Standards Board. In addition, the governor appoints a sheriff and a state's attorney (from a county other than Cook County), a chief of police, and five members of the general public. Members of the ICJIA, other than the Chairman (who is appointed by the governor) do not receive compensation for their service.

The duties of the ICJIA are outlined in 20 ILCS 3930/7, which states that:

> The Authority shall have the following powers, duties and responsibilities:
> (a) To develop and operate comprehensive information systems for the improvement and coordination of all aspects of law enforcement, prosecution and corrections;
> (b) To define, develop, evaluate and correlate State and local programs and projects associated with the improvement of law enforcement and the administration of criminal justice;
> (c) To act as a central repository and clearing house for federal, state and local research studies, plans, projects, proposals and other information relating to all aspects of criminal justice system improvement and to encourage educational programs for citizen support of State and local efforts to make such improvements;
> (d) To undertake research studies to aid in accomplishing its purposes;
> (e) To monitor the operation of existing criminal justice information systems in order to protect the constitutional rights and privacy of individuals about whom criminal history record information has been collected;
> (f) To provide an effective administrative forum for the protection of the rights of individuals concerning criminal history record information;
> (g) To issue regulations, guidelines and procedures which ensure the privacy and security of criminal history record information consistent with State and federal laws;
> (h) To act as the sole administrative appeal body in the State of Illinois to conduct hearings and make final determinations concerning individual challenges to the completeness and accuracy of criminal history record information;
> (i) To act as the sole, official, criminal justice body in the State of Illinois to conduct annual and periodic audits of the procedures, policies, and practices of the State central repositories for criminal history record information to verify compliance with

federal and state laws and regulations governing such information;

(j) To advise the Authority's Statistical Analysis Center;

(k) To apply for, receive, establish priorities for, allocate, disburse and spend grants of funds that are made available by and received on or after January 1, 1983 from private sources or from the United States pursuant to the federal Crime Control Act of 1973, as amended, and similar federal legislation, and to enter into agreements with the United States government to further the purposes of this Act, or as may be required as a condition of obtaining federal funds;

(l) To receive, expend and account for such funds of the State of Illinois as may be made available to further the purposes of this Act;

(m) To enter into contracts and to cooperate with units of general local government or combinations of such units, State agencies, and criminal justice system agencies of other states for the purpose of carrying out the duties of the Authority imposed by this Act or by the federal Crime Control Act of 1973, as amended;

(n) To enter into contracts and cooperate with units of general local government outside of Illinois, other states' agencies, and private organizations outside of Illinois to provide computer software or design that has been developed for the Illinois criminal justice system, or to participate in the cooperative development or design of new software or systems to be used by the Illinois criminal justice system. Revenues received as a result of such arrangements shall be deposited in the Criminal Justice Information Systems Trust Fund.

(o) To establish general policies concerning criminal justice information systems and to promulgate such rules, regulations and procedures as are necessary to the operation of the Authority and to the uniform consideration of appeals and audits;

(p) To advise and to make recommendations to the Governor and the General Assembly on policies relating to criminal justice information systems;

(q) To direct all other agencies under the jurisdiction of the Governor to provide whatever assistance and information the Authority may lawfully require to carry out its functions;

(r) To exercise any other powers that are reasonable and necessary to fulfill the responsibilities of the Authority under this Act and to comply with the requirements of applicable federal law or regulation;

(s) To exercise the rights, powers and duties which have been vested in the Authority by the "Illinois Uniform Conviction Information Act", enacted by the 85th General Assembly, as hereafter amended; and

(t) To exercise the rights, powers and duties which have been vested in the Authority by the Illinois Motor Vehicle Theft Prevention Act.

POLICE TRAINING

Police departments today require highly qualified and well-trained officers. Schmalleger (see pp.229-231) discusses the issue of professionalism and standards in the education and training of police officers.

The Illinois Law Enforcement Training and Standards Board

The **Illinois Law Enforcement Training and Standards Board** (ILETSB) is a state agency which enforces minimum mandatory professional standards for both law enforcement officers and correctional officers in Illinois. The ILETSB sets training standards, ensures that training facilities are adequate, develops training and education programs, and provides financial assistance to departments throughout the state.

The ILETSB, which was created by state statute (50 ILCS 705) has a total of 18 members. These include:

- the Illinois Attorney General
- the Director of State Police
- the Superintendent of the Chicago Police Department
- the Sheriff of Cook County
- the Director of the Illinois Police Training Institute
- the FBI Special Agent in Charge of the Springfield, IL division
- the Executive Director of the Illinois Board of Higher Education

In addition, the governor appoints the following members:

- two mayors or village presidents of Illinois municipalities
- two Illinois county sheriffs from counties other than Cook County
- two managers of Illinois municipalities
- three chiefs of municipal police departments who have no superintendent on the board
- two citizens who meet certain qualifications set forth in 50 ILCS 705/3

According to 50 ILCS 705/6, the ILETSB has the responsibility for selecting and certifying schools in Illinois to provide basic training for probationary police officers, county corrections officers, and court security officers as well as advanced or in-serve training for permanent police or corrections officers. There are a total of six basic law enforcement officers training academies in Illinois which have been approved by ILETSB. They are:

- Belleville Area College Police Academy

- Cook County Sheriff's Police Academy
- Illinois State Police Academy
- Police Training Institute
- Suburban Law Enforcement Academy
- Timothy J. O'Connor Education and Training Center

In addition, the ILETSB has approved four basic correctional officers training academies:

- Cook County Department of Corrections Training Academy
- Cook County Sheriff's Court Services Training Academy
- Police Training Institute
- St. Clair County Sheriff's Correctional Officers Training Academy

The ILETSB's **New Police Chief's Orientation Course** was developed for new chiefs, although individuals who are looking for a position as a chief are also eligible to apply. Topics covered in the course include ethics and integrity, leadership development, politics, unions, collective bargaining, planning and budgetary issues, public safety issues, and many others.

The **Executive Management Program** (EMP) is a training program in law enforcement administration geared for police chiefs, sheriffs, and other top-command level law enforcement personnel. Topics covered in this program include total quality management, negotiating skills, media relations, performance evaluations, community policing, gang control, and many other topics of interest to high-level police administrators.

The ILETSB also has the power to decertify police officers who fail to meet the board's criteria, according to 50 ILCS 705/6.1. No police officer convicted of a felony offense or of certain specified misdemeanor offenses may be certified as a police officer in the State of Illinois. Any officer who has been certified by the ILETSB and who is convicted of any of the offenses outlined in 50 ILCS 705/6.1(a) is immediately decertified.

The Illinois Police Corps Program

Illinois has received funding ($1.2 million in fiscal year 1999) from the United States Office of Justice Programs for the establishment of a **Police Corps Program**, which is housed at Western Illinois University. The program provides college students with federally-funded scholarships to cover tuition, fees, books and supplies, room and board, and transportation. Participants are not required to major in criminal justice or a related field. After completing their bachelor's degree and 24 weeks of Police Corps Academy training, participants will be certified as police officers in Illinois and must serve as community police officers in the state for at least four years.

The Illinois Law Enforcement Intern Training Program

In 1997, Illinois began to allow civilians who were interested in a career in law enforcement to attend the basic training program at a state law enforcement training academy at their own expense. As a result, the **Illinois Law Enforcement Intern Training Program** was developed; it is outlined in 50 ILCS 708.

The selection procedure for the program consists of three steps. The first is the application process and background check. The minimum requirements that must be met by all applicants include:

- minimum age of 21 at start of training
- have a two-year or four-year degree from an accredited college or university or a minimum of sixty hours of general education core requirements
- U.S. citizen
- be eligible for and obtain a Firearm Owners Identification card (F.O.I.D.)
- valid Illinois driver's license
- no felony convictions
- no convictions of crimes of moral turpitude
- no conviction of a domestic violence incident

If the applicant meets all the minimum requirements, the applicant will undergo a thorough background check, including not only the applicant's criminal history but also academic, financial, personal, employment, residency, and driver's license background as well.

Applicants who pass through the first stage of the selection procedure move on to the second phase, which involves a series of five tests or procedures. The first is the P.O.W.E.R. (Peace Officer Wellness Evaluation Report) test, which is a 3.5 hour physical fitness test comprised of four sections, a sit-and-reach test, a one-minute sit-up test, a one-repetition maximum bench press, and a 1.5 mile run. The second procedure involves fingerprinting all applicants as well as a drug screening. The fourth procedure is a one hour cognitive test which looks at reading comprehension, memory, writing skills, and situational judgement. The applicant will also undergo a written psychological evaluation. Those applicants who pass all these tests and procedures are are scheduled for the third step, which is a 45 minute oral interview with a group of law enforcement professionals

The third phase is the academy training period. Applicants accepted to the program attend a minimum of twelve weeks of basic training at a state training academy. Subjects to be studied include (but are not limited to) 30 hours of administrative topics, 82 hours of law, 59 hours of police function and human behavior, 48 hours of patrol, 53 hours of patrol investigations, 42 hours of traffic, 126 hours of firearms and police proficiency training, and 40 hours of integrated exercises. The training program lasts between 400 and 480 hours. Students successfully completing all training requirements will be eligible to take the Illinois State Certification Examination.

Completion of the program does not guarantee the participant a job with a law enforcement agency but the program allows police departments throughout the state to select employees who have already completed the academy training and passed the State Certification Examination.

CHAPTER 5

THE COURT SYSTEM IN ILLINOIS

Schmalleger (see pp.292-306) discusses the general outline of the criminal courts in the United States at both the federal and state levels. The criminal court system in Illinois, as in most states, is a two-tiered system. There are two levels of appellate courts, the Illinois Supreme Court and the Illinois Appellate Courts. In addition, the Illinois Circuit Courts serve as the trial courts of general jurisdiction for the state.

THE HISTORY OF THE ILLINOIS COURT SYSTEM

Illinois was settled by the French in the late 17th century. The first official court known to exist in the area was the **Provincial Council**, established in 1722 to handle both civil and criminal cases. After the Illinois Territory was claimed by Colonel George Rogers Clark as a county of Virginia in 1778, each settlement elected seven men to serve as judges, with a majority of four required for any decision. Colonel Clark himself served as the Court of Appeals. In 1779, the county was reorganized into three districts, each of which had six elected judges who met either monthly or as needed.

In 1787, Illinois became part of the Northwest Territory, which fell under the judicial jurisdiction of a **General Court** consisting of three judges; these judges had both original jurisdiction and served as the Court of Appeals. Minor cases were heard by the **Court of Common Pleas**. The same judicial system was maintained when the Indiana Territory was established in 1800, and later when the Illinois Territory was created in 1809.

In 1814, the **Supreme Court of Illinois** was created. At the same time, the General Court and Court of Common Pleas were abolished in favor of **County Courts**. Individual Supreme Court judges were required to ride circuits and had general jurisdiction in civil and criminal cases.

On December 3, 1818, Illinois became the 21st state of the United States. The judicial system was outlined in Article IV of the state constitution, setting up a Supreme Court with four justices who were appointed by the General Assembly. These judges rode circuit and had original jurisdiction in their circuits over civil and criminal matters. In 1819, the General Assembly established **Justice of the Peace Courts** in each county, giving them county-wide jurisdiction over civil suits up to $100 and over certain criminal cases, primarily those crimes committed by slave or free Negroes.

The 1818 Constitution also gave the General Assembly the power to create **Circuit Courts**, whose jurisdiction was below that of the Supreme Court. In 1824, the General Assembly created five Circuit Courts; these were eliminated in 1827 and the Supreme Court judges returned to riding circuits. However, in 1835, the General Assembly appointed Circuit Court judges for all five circuits (as well as establishing a sixth circuit and judgeship), removing the responsibility of circuit riding from the Supreme Court. The number of circuit courts and circuit court judges increased steadily until there were nine in 1838. This system continued until 1841 when the state judiciary was reorganized and circuit courts and circuit judges were again eliminated by the legislature. The Supreme Court was increased to nine judges who were again assigned Circuit Court duties; this continued until the adoption of the second state constitution in 1848.

Article V of the 1848 Constitution outlined the judicial system of Illinois. The constitution set up a Supreme Court with three judges (two were required for a quorum), one elected from each of the three divisions of the state. This court met once a year in each division and had original jurisdiction in cases of impeachment, habeas corpus, mandamus, and revenue as well as appellate jurisdiction in all other cases. The constitution also established nine circuits, each with a Circuit Court and one elected circuit court judge. The Circuit Court had appellate jurisdiction over all cases on appeal from lower courts and met at least twice a year in each county within the circuit. Each county had a County Court with one judge.

As the population of Illinois increased, the General Assembly created the **Police Magistrate Courts** in each town and city. Cities with no more than 6,000 residents had one police magistrate; those with 6,000 to 12,000 inhabitants had two magistrates, and cities with populations of more than 12,000 had three magistrates. Police Magistrate Courts and Justice of the Peace Courts had concurrent jurisdiction but were not courts of record in the state; appeals were heard as new trials in **Record Courts**, which were also known as **Courts of Common Pleas**. They were located in large cities such as Chicago and Aurora and had concurrent jurisdiction with the Circuit Courts.

The judicial system was again revised with the passage of the Constitution of 1870. The judicial system was outlined in Article VI, which set up a Supreme Court of seven judges. The jurisdiction of the Court was unchanged from the previous Constitution, as was the requirement of annual meetings of the court in each division of the state. However, in 1879, legislation was passed requiring the Court to meet only in Springfield. This legislation also gave the Court the authority to regulate practice for the state judiciary and essentially gave the Court the responsibility for initiating, improving, and interpreting the laws of the state.

Four **Appellate Courts** were established in 1877, as authorized by the Constitution of 1870. Each had three judges appointed by the Supreme Court and the courts had appellate jurisdiction only. Judicial districts were organized in 1873, following the requirements of the new Constitution. A total of 26 circuits were formed; in addition, Cook County formed its own circuit. Each circuit elected Circuit Court judges who held at least two terms of court each year in each county. The circuits were restructured by the Legislature in 1877, reducing the number to thirteen. More changes were made in 1897 and 1957.

The Constitution also called for each county to have a County Court with one elected judge. However, in some cases the General Assembly was allowed to create a district of two or more counties which was under the jurisdiction of one judge.

In counties with a population of over 70,000, the Constitution and later legislation established **Probate Courts**. The Police Magistrates and Justices of the Peace were also continued by the Constitution of 1870. However, these were eliminated in Chicago in 1904 by a constitutional amendment. Later legislation also provided for the establishment of various specialized courts in

Cook County, such as the **Municipal Court of Chicago** and the **Juvenile Court** of Cook County (later known as the **Family Court**).

The **Judicial Article of 1964**, which amended the state constitution, created a unified court system in Illinois. It abolished all trial courts other than Circuit Courts and transferred all their functions, powers, and duties to the various circuit courts. The judicial system of the state was simplified to include a Supreme Court, an Appellate Court, and Circuit Courts. The Supreme Court was comprised of seven judges, to be elected from five judicial districts, with Cook County being the First Judicial District. The rest of the state was divided into four Supreme and Appellate Districts. The Court had original jurisdiction in cases of habeas corpus, mandamus, prohibition, and revenue, and appellate jurisdiction in all other matters. The Court also had general administrative authority over all courts in the state.

The Appellate Courts were organized in the same five judicial districts and had a total of 24 judges. These courts had appellate jurisdiction in all judgements of the Circuit Court except those that were appealable directly to the Supreme Court.

The state was divided into 21 judicial circuits, most of which included several counties. Each circuit had one Circuit Court which had unlimited original jurisdiction. There were three types of judges in Circuit Courts. **Circuit Judges** had full jurisdiction and had the authority to make the rules of the court. **Associate Judges** also had the full jurisdiction of the court but did not have the right to make court rules. Finally, **Magistrates** were appointed by the Circuit judges and were only assigned certain cases, as determined by law. In most courts, they were assigned minor civil and criminal cases, as well as handling internal administrative tasks.

In 1970, the state adopted a new Constitution. Some changes were made to the Judicial Article of 1964, to deal with some of the minor problems that had been found during its seven years in force. Currently, Article VI of the Illinois Constitution, the Judicial Article, provides for a three-tiered judicial system including Circuit Courts, Appellate Courts, and the Supreme Court of Illinois.

UNITED STATES FEDERAL COURTS

Although they are not specifically part of the Florida State Court system, there are three **U.S. District Courts** (see Schmalleger, p.301-302) which sit in Illinois. These are the trial courts of the federal system. The Northern District, which is in Chicago, has 22 authorized judgeships. The Southern District, in East St. Louis, has three authorized judgeships, and the Central District, located in Springfield, also has three authorized judgeships.

The **U.S. Courts of Appeals** (see Schmalleger, pp.302-303) are the intermediate appellate court of the federal court system and have appellate jurisdiction only over federal laws. Judges in these courts are nominated by the President of the United States and confirmed by the Senate. Illinois, along with Indiana and Wisconsin, is part of the Seventh Circuit, which sits in Chicago.

THE ILLINOIS SUPREME COURT

The **Illinois Supreme Court** (see Schmalleger, p.297) is the highest court in the state and is the court of last resort in Illinois. It was created by Article VI of the Illinois State Constitution. The decisions of the Illinois Supreme Court are binding upon all other courts in the state. According to 705 ILCS 5/13:

> The judgments and orders of the supreme court shall be final and conclusive upon all the parties properly before the court.

Seven justices sit on the Illinois Supreme Court, including a Chief Justice and six associate justices. Of these, three must be selected from the First Judicial District (Cook County) and one each from the other four Judicial Districts within the state. The justices are elected and serve terms of ten years. Four justices make up a quorum and at least four justices must agree for a binding decision to be reached. The Chief Justice of the Illinois Supreme Court elected by a majority vote of the justices and serves a three-year term. The Chief Justice has general administrative and supervisory authority over all courts in the state.

Article 6, section 11 of the Illinois State Constitution outlines the requirements necessary to be eligible to serve as a Supreme Court justice. These include:

- be a United States citizen
- be a licensed attorney-at-law of the state of Illinois
- be a resident of the judicial district from which he/she is selected

According to 705 ILCS 55/1 all judges in Illinois must retire at the expiration of the term in which that judge reaches the age of 75. This applies not only to Supreme Court justices, but also to appellate court justices, circuit court judges, and associate judges.

The oath of office to which supreme court judges must swear is outlined in 705 ILCS 5/6:

> I do solemnly swear (or affirm, as the case may be) that I will support the constitution of the United States and the constitution of the state of Illinois, and that I will faithfully discharge the duties of the office of judge of the supreme court of the state of Illinois, according to the best of my ability.

The Supreme Court sits in Springfield. Terms begin on the second Monday in September, November, January, March, and May of each year.

As the final court of appeals in the state, the Supreme Court has a variety of responsibilities. These are outlined in Article VI, Section 4 of the state constitution. The court has original jurisdiction over any cases that relate to revenue, *mandamus*, prohibition, or *habeas corpus*. The court hears appeals from the Appellate Court as a matter of right if there is a question relating to the United States Constitution or the Illinois State Constitution. The court also hears appeals from the Appellate Court if a division of the Appellate Court certifies that the case involves a question that is so important that it needs to be decided by the Supreme Court; in other situations, the court has the discretion to decide whether it will hear appeals from the Appellate Court. In addition, the court hears appeals directly from the Circuit Court when the case resulted in a sentence of death; in other situations, the court has the discretion to allow direct appeal if it so chooses. The Court also has original and exclusive jurisdiction over legislative redistricting and to determine the Governor's ability to serve in office.

ILLINOIS APPELLATE COURTS

The **Appellate Courts** (see Schmalleger, p.297) are Illinois intermediate courts of appeals. The majority of trial court cases which are appealed do not reach the Illinois Supreme Court but are reviewed by the state's appellate courts. The general purpose of an intermediate court of appeals is to serve as a "buffer" between the lower or trial courts and the state supreme court. By handling the majority of the appellate work in the state, appellate courts allow the Supreme Court to review only those cases that raise important legal questions and to ensure that decisions made throughout the state are uniform.

The state is divided into five appellate court districts, with one district court of appeal serving each district. The First Judicial District has 18 appellate judges while the other four each have six appellate judges. The First Judicial District is made up solely of Cook County; the others are multi-county districts. The seat of the Second Judicial District is Elgin, the seat of the Third Judicial District is Ottawa, the seat of the Fourth Judicial District is Springfield, and the seat of the Fifth Judicial District is Mount Vernon. In addition to the 42 appellate court justices required by statute, the Supreme Court may assign additional justices as needed on a temporary basis. In Fiscal Year 1999, there were 42 elected and 10 assigned Appellate Court judges.

The same rules that govern the selection of Supreme Court justices also apply to the selection of Appellate Court judges. Judges are elected and serve ten-year terms. Each Judicial District is divided into appellate divisions, each of which must have at least three judges. Each Judicial District has at least one division; if there is more than one, appellate justices are assigned to individual divisions by the Supreme Court. A majority of the justices in a division makes up a quorum and the agreement of a majority of the division is necessary for a decision to be rendered.

The Appellate Courts hear all appeals from final judgments of the Circuit Courts except for those cases that are directly appealable to the Illinois Supreme Court (such as cases which resulted in a sentence of death). However, there may be no appeal from a Circuit Court judgment of acquittal. Appeals are heard by the appellate court in the district in which the circuit court is located. Decisions are based on the merits of the case; the Appellate Courts do not hear additional testimony or retry the case. The primary purpose of the Appellate Courts is to review the judgement made by the trial court to determine if a legal error was made in applying the law during the Circuit Court trial. If the Appellate Court finds there was no error committed in the application of the law, or if it finds that the error was so minimal that it made little or no difference to the results of the trial, the Court affirms the decision of the trial court. If the Court finds there was a substantive error in the application of the law it will reverse or remand the decision of the trial court and will generally send the case back to the trial court for further action.

In most cases, the decision of the state appellate court represents the final appellate review of a litigated case and is therefore final, although further appeals may be made to either the Illinois Supreme Court or the U.S. Supreme Court. However, neither court is required to hear these appeals and the vast majority of such requests for appeal are denied. In addition, according to 705 ILCS 25/8.1:

> The appellate court may exercise such original jurisdiction as may be necessary to the complete determination of any cause on review.

ILLINOIS CIRCUIT COURTS

Illinois' trial courts of general jurisdiction are known as **Circuit Courts** (see Schmalleger, p.296-297). The state is divided into 22 Judicial Circuits, each of which consists of at least one county. Cook County, the First Judicial District, makes up the Twenty-Second Judicial Circuit; most other judicial circuits are composed of multiple counties. Each Judicial Circuit has one Circuit Court. The Cook County Circuit Court elects a total of 94 circuit judges; the other circuit courts generally elect three or four, depending on the population of the judicial circuit (see 705 ILCS 35/2 for specific details on the number of judges in each judicial circuit).

The same rules that govern the selection of Supreme Court and Appellate Court justices also apply to the selection of Circuit Court judges. Circuit Court judges are elected and serve six year terms. The judges in each circuit elect a Chief Judge who has general administrative authority over the court.

The oath of office to which Circuit Court judges must swear is outlined in 705 ILCS 35/2:

> I do solemnly swear (or affirm, as the case may be) that I will support the constitution of the United States and the constitution of the state of Illinois, and that I will faithfully discharge the duties of the office of judge of ... court, according to the best of my ability.

The Circuit Judges may appoint a number of Associate Judges who serve terms of four years. Although they are not elected, the eligibility requirements for Associate Judges are the same as those for other state judges. Associate Judges may not hear felony cases without prior approval from the state Supreme Court.

Illinois Circuit Courts have original jurisdiction over all cases except those in which the state Supreme Court has original jurisdiction.

COURT ADMINISTRATION

The Illinois Board of Admissions to the Bar

The **Illinois Board of Admissions to the Bar** (IBABY) oversees the administration of state bar admissions. The Board has a total of seven members who are appointed by the Illinois Supreme

Court. All members of IBABY must be members of the Illinois Bar. IBABY is basically an administrative agency of the judicial system with the responsibility of making certain that only qualified individuals are admitted to the practice of law in the state.

IBABY has a variety of functions which revolve around the administration of the process through which individuals who want to be admitted to the state bar show their eligibility. These include:

- the administration of the Illinois Bar Exam twice yearly as a way of identifying and recommending to the Illinois Supreme Court those applicants who are qualified candidates for admission to the Illinois Bar
- the formal investigation of the character and fitness of applicants to the Illinois Bar through the processing of a background investigation
- the review and approval of applicants for admission to the Illinois Bar who have foreign licenses.

Final appointment to the Illinois Bar is done by the Illinois Supreme Court, not the Illinois Board of Admissions to the Bar.

The Illinois Judicial Inquiry Board

Article VI, Section 15b of the Illinois Constitution created a **Judicial Inquiry Board**. The board has a total of nine members. Of these, two are Circuit Court Judges appointed by the Supreme Court, three are lawyers appointed by the governor, and four are non-lawyers appointed by the governor. Board members serve for terms of four years and may not serve more than two terms. The Board designates a Chair and Vice-Chair, each of whom serve terms of one year. The Chair serves as the chief executive of the Board; the Vice-Chair performs these duties in the absence of the Chair.

The Judicial Inquiry Board receives or initiates complaints regarding any allegations of misconduct or physical or mental incapacity of judges (including associate judges) in Illinois. The Board investigates these allegations and, if they feel there is a reasonable basis to charge a judge with incapacity or misconduct, the Board files and prosecutes a formal complaint with the **Illinois Courts Commission**. According to Article VI, Section 15c of the Constitution:

> The Board shall not file a complaint unless five members believe that a reasonable basis exists
> (1) to charge the Judge or Associate Judge with willful misconduct in office, persistent failure to perform his duties, or other conduct that is prejudicial to the administration of justice or that brings the judicial office into disrepute, or
> (2) to charge that the Judge or Associate Judge is physically or mentally unable to perform his duties. All proceedings of the Board shall be confidential except the filing of a complaint with the Courts Commission. The Board shall prosecute the complaint.

During Fiscal Year 1999, the Board initiated or received a total of 447 complaints against judges which were filed by citizens, attorneys, and other judges. Some judges had multiple complaints filed against them. Of the complaints, 40 were against Supreme Court and Appellate Court Judges, 246 were against Circuit Court Judges, 159 were against Circuit Court Associate Judges, and 2 were against candidates for election to a judicial position.

The Illinois Courts Commission

The **Illinois Courts Commission** was created by Article VI, Section 15e of the Illinois Constitution. The Commission has a total of seven members (not counting alternates), including:

> one Supreme Court Judge selected by that Court as a member and one as an alternate, two Appellate Court Judges selected by that Court as members and three as alternates, two Circuit Judges selected by the Supreme Court as members and three as alternates, and two citizens selected by the Governor as members and two as alternates. Members and alternates who are Appellate Court Judges must each be from a different Judicial District. Members and alternates who are Circuit Judges must each be from a different Judicial District. Members and alternates of the Commission shall not be members of the Judicial Inquiry Board.

The members select an individual from among their number to serve a two-year term as Commission Chair.

The purpose of the Commission is to hear complaints that have been filed against state judges or associate judges by the Judicial Inquiry Board. The Courts Commission is not part of the Judicial Inquiry Board; it is a separate body. It may only hear a complaint against a judge if the Judicial Inquiry Board has investigated the allegation and filed a formal complaint. In these cases, the Board acts as the prosecutor in the Commission proceedings. If the complaint is sustained, the Commission may impose one of four penalties on a judge or associate judge:

- it may reprimand the judge or associate judge
- it may censure the judge or associate judge
- it may suspend the judge or associate judge without pay
- it may remove the judge or associate judge from office

In addition, if the complaint revolves around the physical or mental inability of the judge or associate judge to perform his or her duties, the Commission may suspend (with or without pay) or retire the judge or associate judge.

All Commission decisions are final. The agreement of at least four members of the Commission is required for a decision to be reached.

ILLINOIS CRIMINAL COURT PROCEDURES

Schmalleger (see pp.16-20, pp.306-314, and pp.339-353) outlines the basic procedures involved in a criminal trial, including the pretrial activities. The specific procedures used in the Illinois court system are extremely similar to those discussed in Schmalleger. The criminal justice process beings when the police are notified (or in some other way discover) that a crime has been committed and initiate an investigation into that crime. The discussion in this section will focus primarily upon the procedures for felony cases. The procedures for misdemeanors are similar, although some stages are omitted from the process.

Arrest and Booking

After the police have determined both that a crime has in fact been committed and that a specific person committed the crime, they may place that individual under **arrest**. Schmalleger discusses the issue of arrest briefly on p.16 and in detail on pp.258-259. In Illinois, an arrest is defined in 725 ILCS 5/102-5 as "the taking of a person into custody." In some situations, the police may have obtained an **arrest warrant** from a judge; 725 ILCS 5/107-1 defines a warrant of arrest as:

> a written order from a court directed to a peace officer, or to some other person specifically named, commanding him to arrest a person.

In Illinois, for a law enforcement officer to arrest a specific individual, the officer must have a warrant of arrest unless:

- he/she has reasonable grounds to believe that a warrant for the arrest of that individual has been issued either in Illinois or in another jurisdiction

- he/she has reasonable grounds to believe that the individual is committing or has committed an offense (e.g., the individual committed or attempted to commit a crime in the officer's presence)

After a suspect has been arrested and taken to the county jail, he/she undergoes the **booking** procedure (see Schmalleger, p.16), which involves entering into the police record various facts about the suspect. At this time, the suspect will be photographed and fingerprinted and may be placed in a police lineup.

Bond Hearing

After a felony offender has been arrested and booked, he/she goes through a bond hearing. At this hearing, which is the offenders' first appearance before a judge, the court decides whether the defendant is entitled to any form of **pretrial release**, including **bail** (see Schmalleger, pp.307-310). Although the U.S. Supreme Court stated in *Stack v. Boyle* that the U.S. Constitution does not guarantee the right to bail, the Illinois State Constitution and the state criminal code do provide a substantive right to bail in many cases.

According to 725 ILCS 5/110-4(a):

> All persons shall be bailable before conviction, except the following offenses where the proof is evident or the presumption great that the defendant is guilty of the offense: capital offenses; offenses for which a sentence of life imprisonment may be imposed as a consequence of conviction; felony offenses for which a sentence of imprisonment, without conditional and revocable release, shall be imposed by law as

a consequence of conviction, where the court after a hearing, determines that the release of the defendant would pose a real and present threat to the physical safety of any person or persons; stalking or aggravated stalking, where the court, after a hearing, determines that the release of the defendant would pose a real and present threat to the physical safety of the alleged victim of the offense and denial of bail is necessary to prevent fulfillment of the threat upon which the charge is based; or unlawful use of weapons ... when that offense occurred in a school or in any conveyance owned, leased, or contracted by a school to transport students to or from school or a school-related activity, or on any public way within 1,000 feet of real property comprising any school, where the court, after a hearing, determines that the release of the defendant would pose a real and present threat to the physical safety of any person and denial of bail is necessary to prevent fulfillment of that threat.

In addition, the court has the option of ordering that the individual be **released on his/her own personal recognizance**, if the court believes the defendant will appear before the court as required, will not pose a danger to anyone in the community, and will comply with all conditions of release. This issue is discussed in 725 ILCS 5/110-2 (see Schmalleger, p.308).

In Illinois, if an individual is granted any form of pretrial release (either bail or on recognizance), the conditions of the release will include according to 725 ILCS 5/110-10(a), the requirements that the individual will:

(1) Appear to answer the charge in the court having jurisdiction on a day certain and thereafter as ordered by the court until discharged or final order of the court;
(2) Submit himself or herself to the orders and process of the court;
(3) Not depart this State without leave of the court;
(4) Not violate any criminal statute of any jurisdiction;
(5) At a time and place designated by the court, surrender all firearms in his or her possession to a law enforcement officer designated by the court to take custody of and impound the firearms when the offense the person has been charged with is a forcible felony, stalking, aggravated stalking, domestic battery, any violation of either the Illinois Controlled Substances Act or the Cannabis Control Act that is classified as a Class 2 or greater felony, or any felony violation of Article 24 of the Criminal Code of 1961..; and
(6) At a time and place designated by the court, submit to a psychological evaluation when the person has been charged with a violation of item (4) of subsection (a) of Section 24-1 of the Criminal Code of 1961 and that violation occurred in a school or in any conveyance owned, leased, or contracted by a school to transport students to or from school or a school-related activity, or on any public way within 1,000 feet of real property comprising any school ... As a further condition of bail under these circumstances, the court shall order the defendant to refrain from entering upon the property of the school, including any conveyance owned, leased, or contracted by a school to transport students to or from school or a school-related activity, or on any public way within 1,000 feet of real property comprising any school.

Preliminary Hearing or Examination

In most cases, a felony offender will have a **preliminary hearing** or **preliminary examination** (the two terms appear to be used interchangeably in the ILCS.) During the preliminary hearing (see Schmalleger, p.18 and pp.306-307), the judge formally provides the defendant with several important pieces of information, including the nature of the charge against him or her. The defendant is also given a copy of the charge. The judge is also required by statute to advise defendants of their right to counsel. At this time, if the defendant is indigent and cannot afford to hire an attorney, the court will appoint counsel (see Schmalleger, pp.328-330). The defendant has the right to waive the preliminary hearing; in addition, if the defendant has been indicted by a Grand Jury, he/she does not go through a preliminary hearing.

During the preliminary hearing, the judge determines whether there is probable cause to believe that an offense was committed by the defendant. If the judge returns a finding of probable cause, the prosecution enters a formal indictment before the court. If the judge returns a finding of no probable cause, the prosecution has the option of brining the case before a Grand Jury as well.

The Grand Jury and Indictment

According to Article I, Section 7 of the Illinois State Constitution,

> No person shall be held to answer for a crime punishable by death or by imprisonment in the penitentiary unless either the initial charge has been brought by indictment of a grand jury or the person has been given a prompt preliminary hearing to establish probable cause.

725 ILCS 112 discusses the procedures relating to the **grand jury** (see Schmalleger, p.311). The purpose of the grand jury is to determine whether or not there is sufficient evidence to justify a formal indictment against the accused individual. If the grand jury decides that the evidence constitutes probable cause to believe that a crime has been committed by the accused, a **Bill of Indictment** is prepared, charging the accused with the offense. If the grand jury finds that there is insufficient evidence to show that the accused individual committed the crime, a **No Bill** will be issued and the case dismissed.

In Illinois, the grand jury is composed of 16 individuals, of which 12 constitutes a quorum. Individuals appearing before the grand jury have the right to counsel. However, the counsel may only advise the individual of his/her rights; counsel may not participate in any other way in the proceedings of the grand jury.

Arraignment and Plea

The next stage in the criminal process is the **arraignment** (see Schmalleger, p.19 and p.312). According to 725 ILCS 113-1,

> Before any person is tried for the commission of an offense he shall be called into open court, informed of the charge against him, and called upon to plead thereto. If

the defendant so requests the formal charge shall be read to him before he is required to plead. An entry of the arraignment shall be made of record.

The arraignment generally occurs three weeks from the date of the information or indictment. During the arraignment, the defendant enters a **plea** (see Schmalleger, p.19 and p.312). 725 ILCS 5/113-4 outlines the various plea options that the defendant has at this stage. In nearly every case, the defendant will plead "not guilty" at the arraignment. However, he/she does have the option of pleading "guilty" or "guilty but mentally ill." If the defendant stands mute and refuses to plea, a plea of not guilty is entered. If the defendant chooses to plead guilty at the arraignment, the judge has the option of refusing the plea if the judge is not certain that the defendant understands what he/she is doing and what the consequences of such a plea may be. If a defendant enters a plea of guilty, he/she waives the right to a trial and proceeds directly to the sentencing phase of the criminal court procedures.

Discovery

After the arraignment, both sides engage in a reciprocal **discovery process** (see Schmalleger, p.18 and p.347). The discovery process is outlined in detail in the Article IV, Part B of the Supreme Court Rules (S. Ct. Rule). These rules apply in all criminal cases which could result in the defendant receiving a sentence of imprisonment in a state penitentiary (effectively, all felony cases).

In general, the prosecution files their answer to discovery first, disclosing information to the accused. According to S.Ct. Rule 412, the material disclosed to the defense includes the following:

- the names and addresses of all individuals the prosecution intends to call as witnesses, along with any statements made by these individuals
- any statements made by the defendant (and/or any codefendants) and a list of any witnesses to these statements
- a transcript of the portions of grand jury minutes that contain testimony by the defendant or any persons the prosecution intends to call as witnesses
- any reports or statements by experts, along with a statement of the qualifications of the expert
- any books, papers, documents, photographs, or other tangible objects that were obtained from the defendant or that belong to the defendant or that the prosecution intends to use at trial
- any record of prior criminal convictions of persons the state intends to call as witnesses
- whether there was any electronic surveillance (e.g., wiretapping) used against the defendant
- any material or information the state has that tends to negate the accused's guilt or reduce his/her punishment

Because Illinois' discovery process is reciprocal, not only does the prosecution provide the defendant with information, but the defense is also be required to provide certain information to the prosecution. According to S. Ct. Rule 413, the defense must disclose to the prosecution:

- the person of the accused — the accused may be required to appear in a lineup, speak to witnesses for identification purposes, be fingerprinted, pose for photographs, try on specific articles of clothing, permit the taking of samples of bodily fluids, hair, etc., provide a handwriting sample, and submit to a reasonable physical or medical inspection of his/her body
- medical and scientific reports of any physical or mental examinations or of any scientific tests or comparisons, or any other reports or statements of experts
- any defenses that the defense counsel intends to make at trial

Plea Bargaining

Schmalleger (see pp.312-314) discusses the issue of plea bargaining in detail. While plea bargaining is not a formal stage of the criminal justice process, it is an extremely important process in every state, including Illinois. The plea bargaining process may take place throughout the pre-trial process and even continue during the trial itself. Generally, plea bargains are not made until after the arraignment and discovery.

During the plea bargaining process, the prosecutor negotiates with the defense attorney (or the defendant). The purpose of the negotiation is to reach an agreement whereby the defendant will enter a plea of guilty, generally in exchange for either a reduced charge or a recommendation to the court of a lenient sentence. The defense attorney is responsible for advising the defendant of all plea offers and any other relevant matters that may affect the defendant's decision (e.g., the possible results of each plea). The defense attorney may not accept any plea bargain without the full consent of the defendant.

The judge does not participate directly in plea bargaining but he/she is an extremely important element in the process because he/she must accept the plea. After the defense and the prosecution have reached a mutually acceptable plea, the agreement must be presented to the judge. The judge has to approve the plea; he/she is not required to accept the defendant's plea of guilty. Generally, the judge will refuse to accept a guilty plea in the following situations:

- the judge feels that the plea is not appropriate
- the judge feels that the defendant does not understand what he/she is pleading guilty to and what the agreement is
- the judge feels that the defendant does not understand the consequences of his/her plea of guilty

Pre-Trial Motions

There are a number of **pre-trial motions** that may be filed in Illinois (see Schmalleger, pp.347-348). A **motion to dismiss** is filed by the defense and asks the court to dismiss the indictment on one of the grounds outlined in 725 ILCS 5/114-1. A **motion for continuance** (see 725 ILCS 5/114-4) may be filed by either the defense or the prosecution. It requests that the case be delayed for a specific period of time. Reasons for requesting a continuance include (but are not limited to) the illness or death of defense counsel, the illness or death of the prosecutor assigned to the case, the unavailability of a material witness, or the physical or mental incompetency of the defendant.

A **motion to suppress evidence illegally seized** (see 725 ILCS 5/114-12) claims that evidence was obtained through an unlawful search and seizure and should therefore be prohibited for use as evidence in court. This motion generally applies to physical evidence. To suppress testimonial evidence, the defendant must file a **motion to suppress a confession** (see 725 ILCS 5/114-11). This motion claims that a confession or admission made by the defendant was not voluntary and thus was obtained illegally.

Other pre-trial motions that may be filed include a **motion for a bill of particulars** (see 725 ILCS 5/114-2), a **motion to discharge jury panel** (see 725 ILCS 5/114-3), a **motion for the substitution of judge** (see 725 ILCS 5/114-5), a motion for a **change of place of trial** (see 725 ILCS 5/114-6), a **joinder of related prosecutions** (see 725 ILCS 5/114-7), a **motion for severance** (see ILCS 5/114-8), a **motion for a list of witnesses** (see 725 ILCS 5/114-8), and a **motion to produce confession** (see 725 ILCS 5/114-9).

The Right to a Speedy Trial

Schmalleger (see pp.341-342) discusses the constitutional right to a **speedy trial**. The Illinois State Constitution also provides for the right to a speedy trial (Article I, Section 8). Each case must be brought to trial within a certain specified period of time. In general, an offender held in custody must be tried within 120 days of the date he/she was taken into custody. If the individual is on bail or on recognizance, he/she must be tried within 160 days. However, if the defendant is responsible for delays in bringing the case to trial, these delay periods are not included in the maximum pre-trial period.

If the defendant has not been brought to trial within the prescribed period of crime, he/she must be released from custody or released from the obligations of his/her bail or recognizance.

Trial

Less than ten percent of all felony and misdemeanor cases go to a formal criminal **trial** (see Schmalleger, pp.19-20); the vast majority are disposed of by a plea of guilty on the part of the defendant. If the defendant enters a plea of not guilty and the case does go to trial, the procedure is the same regardless of whether the case involves a felony or a misdemeanor.

According to both the Sixth Amendment to the U.S. Constitution and the Illinois State Constitution (Article I, Section 16), all defendants have the right to a speedy and public trial before an impartial jury. However, if the defendant chooses to to waive his/her right to a **jury trial** he/she will be given a **bench trial** (see Schmalleger, p.20). A bench trial is held before a judge but there is no jury present.

Jury Selection
The first step in a jury trial is the **selection of the jury**. Illinois uses a twelve-member jury. A list of prospective jurors is chosen at random from the lists of registered voters and licensed drivers in the county in which the trial is being held.

Schmalleger (see pp.342-345) discusses the topic of jury selection in detail. As noted in Schmalleger (see p.342), the process of jury selection is known as *voir dire* and involves an examination of the prospective jurors by the court and by the attorneys for both the prosecution and the defense. The stated purpose of the voir dire is to determine whether each potential juror is impartial and will be able to render a fair verdict in a case. Potential jurors are placed under oath and then questioned by the judge, prosecutor, and defense counsel.

During the process, both the defense and prosecutor are allowed to make challenges, or to object to the inclusion of certain potential trial jurors. Illinois allows two types of challenges. **Challenges for cause** (see Schmalleger p.342) generally are based on the attorney's belief that the juror is biased in some way that will prevent him or her from acting impartially and without prejudice during the trial. According to 725 ILCS 5/115-4(d):

> Each party may challenge jurors for cause. If a prospective juror has a physical impairment, the court shall consider such prospective juror's ability to perceive and appreciate the evidence when considering a challenge for cause.

Peremptory challenges (see Schmalleger, p.342 and p.346) may be used by either attorney to remove potential jurors from the jury panel without giving any specific reasons. According to 725 ILCS 5/115-4(e), the number of peremptory challenges allowed depends on the charge(s) against the defendant:

> A defendant tried alone shall be allowed 20 peremptory challenges in a capital case, 10 in a case in which the punishment may be imprisonment in the penitentiary, and 5 in all other cases; except that, in a single trial of more than one defendant, each defendant shall be allowed 12 peremptory challenges in a capital case, 6 in a case in which the punishment may be imprisonment in the penitentiary, and 3 in all other cases. If several charges against a defendant or defendants are consolidated for trial, each defendant shall be allowed peremptory challenges upon one charge only, which single charge shall be the charge against that defendant authorizing the greatest maximum penalty. The State shall be allowed the same number of peremptory challenges as all of the defendants.

After the selection of the jury is completed, the jurors are **impaneled** and **sworn in by the court** (see Schmalleger, p.345). The court may then direct the selection of two alternate jurors; the defense and the prosecution are each given one additional peremptory challenge for each alternate juror.

Opening Statements
Schmalleger (see p.345 and p.349) discusses the use of **opening statements**. Both the prosecutor and the defense attorney are entitled to make an opening statement which provides all the participants in the trial, especially the jury, with an overview of the facts of the case. However, such statements are optional and neither side is required to make an opening statement. In Illinois, the prosecutor always makes the first statement. After the prosecution's opening remarks are completed, the defense has the option of making an opening statement or may choose to wait until the start of the defense case. In the case of a bench trial, both the defense and the prosecutor generally waive their right to an opening statement.

Presentation of the Prosecution's Evidence
After the opening statements are completed, the prosecution begins to present evidence in support of the charge that has been brought against the defendant. The prosecution presents first because the state is bringing the charge against the defendant and, because of the presumption of innocence, has assumed the burden of proof. Evidence submitted into court may include documents, pictures, recordings, depositions, objects, pictures, or witness testimony (see Schmalleger, pp.349-352 for a discussion of various types of evidence).

The prosecutor generally begins with **direct examination** of the prosecution's first witness, who is obviously expected to give evidence to support the state's case against the defendant. After the prosecutor finishes questioning the witness, the defense is allowed to **cross-examine** the same witness. If the prosecutor wishes, he/she may then return to ask the witness more questions in a process is known as **re-direct examination**. Following this, the defense attorney has the option to question the witness once more during the **re-cross examination**. The procedure may continue with **re-re-direct** and **re-re-cross** but this is rare. This procedure is repeated for each witness called by the prosecution.

Presentation of the Defense's Evidence
After the prosecution has presented all its evidence and called all its witnesses, the defense may then offer evidence. Because the defendant is considered to be innocent until proven guilty, and because the burden of proof to prove the defendant's guilt is upon the prosecution, the defense is not required to offer any evidence or call any witnesses. The defendant is not required to testify at any point in the trial; both the U.S. Constitution and the Illinois State Constitution specifically protect the defendant against self-incrimination. The procedure for the presentation of the evidence by the defense is similar to that of the prosecution: direct examination, cross examination, re-direct, and re-cross.

Rebuttal and Surrebuttal
After the defense has presented its evidence, the prosecution is entitled to present a **rebuttal** case. At this time, the prosecutor may present evidence in response to the case presented by the defense. The defense may also be entitled to present a **surrebuttal** case, which involves presenting evidence after the prosecution has completed the rebuttal. However, this is at the discretion of the trial court.

Closing Arguments
Once all the evidence is presented, each side is given the opportunity to make a **closing argument** which is addressed directly to the jury (see Schmalleger, pp.352-353). During this stage of the trial, each attorney reviews and summarizes the evidence that best supports their side of case, discusses any inferences that may be drawn from that evidence, and points out weaknesses in the opponent's case. In Illinois, the prosecution makes its closing arguments first, followed by the defense. The prosecution is then given an opportunity for rebuttal.

Instructions to the Jury
After the closing arguments are completed, the judge has the opportunity to provide instructions to the jury regarding any legal issues or points of law which are applicable to the case. This step is also known as **charging the jury** (see Schmalleger, p.353).

Jury Deliberation and Verdict Rendition
After the judge has given instructions to the jury, the jury retires to the jury room for **deliberation** (see Schmalleger, p.353). At this time, the jurors discuss the case and attempt to come to agreement on a **verdict** concerning the guilt or innocence of the defendant. Illinois law requires that all jurors agree on a guilty verdict before the defendant can be convicted of the charge. If the jurors are unable to agree on a verdict after a reasonable period of time, they are **deadlocked** and considered to be a "**hung jury**." If this happens, the judge will declare a **mistrial** and the case may have to be retried in front of a new jury.

If the jurors come to an agreement on a verdict, they return to the courtroom and the verdict is read aloud in open court.

If the verdict of the jury is not guilty, the trial is over and the defendant must be immediately discharged from custody and is entitled to the return of any bail money and the exoneration of any sureties. The trial court judge is required to accept a verdict of not guilty. Because of the state and federal constitutional protections against double jeopardy, the defendant may never be tried in state court for those same charges.

Proceedings Between the Verdict and the Sentence
If the defendant is found guilty, he/she will be sentenced. However, after a verdict of guilty is rendered and before the sentencing phase of the trial, the defendant may make one or more **post-trial motions** (see Schmalleger, pp.347-348). These may include a **motion for a new trial** (see 725 ILCS 5/116-1) or a **motion in arrest of judgment** (see 725 ILCS 5/116-2). These motions are rarely granted.

The Sentence
If the defendant is found guilty, he/she will be sentenced by a judge. In Illinois, the **sentence** is pronounced by the trial judge; there is no separate sentencing hearing. See Schmalleger (p.20) for a brief overview of sentencing and Chapter 10 of Schmalleger for a more in-depth discussion.

Illinois has a determinate sentencing policy; the possible sentence depends upon the offense at conviction. Authorized sentences are outlined in 730 ILCS 5 and include probation, periodic imprisonment, conditional discharge, imprisonment, fines, restitution, and death. In the case of sentences of imprisonment, the statutes provide a range, a minimum and maximum terms. For example, according to 730 ILCS 5/5-8-1(a)(1.5), the term of imprisonment for second degree murder shall be not less than 4 years and not more than 20 years. The length of the sentence within the maximum and minimum terms is determined by the judge who takes into account the presence of various mitigating factors (as outlined in 730 ILCS 5/5-5-3.1) and/or aggravating factors (as outlined in 730 ILCS 5/5/5-3.2).

The sentencing process is discussed in more detail in the next chapter.

Appeal
If the defendant is convicted of a crime, he/she may have the option of **appealing** the conviction (see Schmalleger, p.297). An appeal does not involve retrying a case or re-examining the factual issues surrounding the crime; it only involves an examination or review of the legal issues involved in the

case. The purpose of an appeal is to make certain that the defendant received a fair trial and that he/she was not deprived of any constitutional rights at any time. In most cases, if a defendant wins on appeal, he/she will be retried.

CHAPTER 6

SENTENCING IN ILLINOIS

INTRODUCTION

After a criminal defendant pleads guilty or is found guilty in court by a judge or jury, the judge must impose a sentence of punishment upon the offender. A **sentence** is defined in 730 ILCS 5/5-1-19 as "the disposition imposed by the court on a convicted defendant." The general philosophy of sentencing, including the justification and aims of punishment is discussed in Schmalleger (see pp.365-369).

In every case in which a conviction has been entered, the court is required to pronounce sentence. If the defendant has been found guilty on multiple counts, the court must pronounce sentence on each count. In most cases, the final sentence is determined by the judge. However, in those cases where the defendant has been convicted of a capital crime, the defendant has the choice whether or not to have a jury participate in the sentencing process.

TYPES OF SENTENCES

A variety of sentences may be imposed upon convicted offenders in Illinois (see Schmalleger, p.386). According to 730 ILCS 5/5-5-3, dispositions that are acceptable in the Illinois courts include:

- a period of probation
- a term of periodic imprisonment
- a term of conditional discharge
- a term of imprisonment
- a fine
- restitution to the victim
- participation in a county impact incarceration program
- death (for first degree murder only)

In many cases, combinations of these dispositions are also acceptable. For example, a judge may sentence an offender to both imprisonment and a fine, or order an offender to serve a period of probation as well as making restitution to the victim. However, the statute also limits the use of some of these dispositions. For example, the statute lists a number of offenses for which the court may not impose a sentence of probation, periodic imprisonment, or conditional discharge. For these crimes, the court must impose a sentence of imprisonment, although a fine or restitution may be ordered as well.

Misdemeanors are classified as Class A, Class B, and Class C. Sentences of imprisonment for misdemeanor offenses are outlined in 730 ILCS 5/5-8-3. Authorized fines for misdemeanors are discussed in 730 ILCS 5/5-9-1. Authorized periods of probation and conditional discharge for misdemeanors are outlined in 730 ILCS 5/5-6-2.

WHEN SENTENCING OCCURS

The Presentence Investigation

If a defendant enters a plea of guilty at the arraignment, and it is accepted by the judge, there is no trial and the court proceeds directly to the sentencing phase. If the defendant enters a plea of not guilty and is then found guilty in a criminal trial, the sentence may be imposed by the court immediately following the trial or in a sentencing hearing scheduled for a later date.

According to 730 ILCS 5/5-3-1:

> A defendant shall not be sentenced for a felony before a written presentence report of investigation is presented to and considered by the court.
>
> However, the court need not order a presentence report of investigation where both parties agree to the imposition of a specific sentence, provided there is a finding made for the record as to the defendant's history of delinquency or criminality, including any previous sentence to a term of probation, periodic imprisonment, conditional discharge, or imprisonment.
>
> The court may order a presentence investigation of any defendant.

Thus, unless the court has agreed to a plea bargain that includes agreement as to the specific sentence, the court must obtain a **presentence investigation** (see Schmalleger, pp.379 and 381) for all felony offenders. The court has the option of ordering such an investigation for misdemeanor offenders but this is not mandatory.

The presentence report contains a variety of information about the offender's background and about the circumstances of the crime. According to 730 ILCS 5/5-3-2(a), a presentence report must include:

> (1) the defendant's history of delinquency or criminality, physical and mental history and condition, family situation and background, economic status, education, occupation and personal habits;
> (2) information about special resources within the community which might be available to assist the defendant's rehabilitation...
> (3) the effect the offense committed has had upon the victim or victims thereof, and any compensatory benefit that various sentencing alternatives would confer on such victim or victims;
> (4) information concerning the defendant's status since arrest, including his record if released on his own recognizance, or the defendant's achievement record if released on a conditional pre-trial supervision program;

(5) when appropriate, a plan, based upon the personal, economic and social adjustment needs of the defendant, utilizing public and private community resources as an alternative to institutional sentencing;

(6) any other matters that the investigatory officer deems relevant or the court directs to be included; and

(7) information concerning defendant's eligibility for a sentence to a county impact incarceration program...

The court also has the option of ordering a physical and/or mental examination of the defendant.

If the offender is convicted of a misdemeanor, the presentence report must contain information on the defendant's history of criminal or delinquent behavior. If the court requests, the report may also contain information on the first six items found in the felony report; however, a misdemeanor report will not include information concerning whether the defendant is eligible for sentence to a county impact incarceration program.

The Sentencing Hearing

The **sentencing hearing** is discussed in 730 ILCS 5/5-4-1, which states that:

> Except when the death penalty is sought under hearing procedures otherwise specified, after a determination of guilt, a hearing shall be held to impose the sentence.

At this hearing, the judge must consider a variety of factors, including:

- any evidence that was received at trial
- any presentence reports provided to the court
- the financial impact of incarceration (this is based on a financial impact statement that the Department of Corrections files with the clerk of the court)
- any evidence and information offered in aggravation and/or mitigation
- any arguments regarding sentencing alternatives

In addition, during the hearing, the judge must give the defendant the opportunity to make a statement in his/her own behalf, although the defendant is not required to do so. In the case of a violent crime, and in certain traffic-related offenses, the judge must also give the victim an opportunity to make a statement regarding the impact the crime has had on him/her and to present evidence in aggravation or mitigation. However, this statement and evidence must be prepared with the State's Attorney before it may be presented orally at the sentencing hearing. If the crime is one of reckless homicide, the victim's spouse, parents, guardian, or other immediate family must be given the opportunity to make oral statements.

Sentences are imposed by the judge after due consideration of these factors. The judge imposing the sentence is generally the same judge who accepted the defendant's plea of guilty or who presided at the trial at which the defendant was adjudicated guilty.

DETERMINATE AND INDETERMINATE SENTENCING

Schmalleger (see pp.371-374) discusses the concept of **structured** or **determinate sentencing**. A determinate sentence is a flat or fixed-term prison sentence for an offense. In other words, rather than passing a sentence that includes a range of time to be served in prison (for example, three to five years in the state prison), the sentence is a fixed period of time (for example, four years in prison). A sentence that includes a range of time between a specified minimum and maximum is known as an **indeterminate sentence** (see Schmalleger, pp.369-371).

In Illinois, all felony offenders who are sentenced to a term of imprisonment receive a determinate sentence. Illinois does not use indeterminate sentences. Thus, although, for example, the statutory sentence of imprisonment for second degree murder is a term of not less than four nor more than 20 years, the court must sentence the offender to a specific fixed period of time within that range. The judge may not sentence the offender to a sentence of four to six years.

CONCURRENT VERSUS CONSECUTIVE SENTENCES

If an offender is convicted of multiple offenses, the court may impose a sentence for each offense. If the sentences imposed involve terms of imprisonment in either a county jail or a state prison, the court has the option of requiring the sentences to be served concurrently or consecutively. **Concurrent sentences** are served at the same time. **Consecutive sentences** are served in succession, one after the other (see Schmalleger, p.20).

In most situations, the court has considerable discretion in deciding whether multiple sentences will be served concurrently or consecutively. However, in some circumstances, the law sets forth specific requirements and removes the discretion from the court. For example, 730 ILCS 5/5-8-4 states that:

> The court shall not impose consecutive sentences for offenses which were committed as part of a single course of conduct during which there was no substantial change in the nature of the criminal objective, unless:
> (i) one of the offenses for which defendant was convicted was a Class X or Class 1 felony and the defendant inflicted severe bodily injury, or
> (ii) the defendant was convicted of a violation of Section 12-13, 12-14, or 12-14.1 of the Criminal Code of 1961, or
> (iii) the defendant was convicted of armed violence based upon the predicate offense of solicitation of murder, solicitation of murder for hire, heinous battery, aggravated battery of a senior citizen, criminal sexual assault, a violation of subsection (g) of Section 5 of the Cannabis Control Act, cannabis trafficking, a violation of subsection (a) of Section 401 of the Illinois Controlled Substances Act, controlled substance trafficking involving a Class X felony amount of controlled substance under Section 401 of the Illinois Controlled Substances Act, calculated criminal drug conspiracy, or streetgang criminal drug conspiracy,
> in which event the court shall enter sentences to run consecutively. Sentences shall run concurrently unless otherwise specified by the court.

SENTENCES OF INCARCERATION

Felony Sentences

All felonies defined in the Illinois Compiled Statutes include a classification into a "Class." Felonies other than first degree murder may fall into one of five categories: Class X, Class 1, Class 2, Class 3, or Class 4. The specific sentences of incarceration for each class are outlined in 730 ILCS 5/5-8-1. Authorized fines for each felony class are discussed in 730 ILCS 5/5-9-1; in all cases (and for the crime of first degree murder), the maximum authorized fine is $25,000. A fine may be required in addition to a term of imprisonment or the offender may receive a sentence that includes payment of a fine but no incarceration. In addition, 730 ILCS 5/5-8-2 discusses the concept of **extended terms** of incarceration; an offender may only be sentenced extended term of imprisonment if one or more aggravating factors were found to be present. Authorized periods of probation and conditional discharge for felony offenses are outlined in 730 ILCS 5/5-6-2.

There are a number of exceptions to this. For example, second degree murder is a Class 1 felony in Illinois. However, 730 ILCS 5/5-8-1(a)(1.5) outlines a specific period of incarceration for this crime that is different from the standard term for Class 1 felonies. In addition, first degree murder does not fall into any of the above five categories. The authorized penalties for first degree murder include a term of imprisonment of not less than 20 nor more than 60 years, a term of natural life imprisonment, or a sentence of death. The extended term for this crime is a term of incarceration of between 60 and 100 years.

Class X felonies include, but are not limited to: aggravated criminal sexual assault, armed robbery, henious battery, aggravated arson, and aggravated vehicular hijacking. An offender who is convicted of a Class X felony may be sentenced to a period of imprisonment of at least six years but no more than 30 years. If one or more aggravating factors are present, the offender may be sentenced to an extended term of not less than 30 but not more than 60 years.

Class 1 felonies include, among other crimes, vehicular hijacking, criminal sexual assault, aggravated robbery, residential burglary, and residential arson. An offender who is convicted of a Class 1 felony may be sentenced to a period of imprisonment of at least four years but no more than 30 years. If one or more aggravating factors are present, the offender may be sentenced to an extended term of not less than 15 but not more than 30 years.

Class 2 felonies include, but are not limited to, robbery, burglary, and simple arson. Offenders convicted of a Class 2 felony may be sentenced to a term of imprisonment of not more than three nor less than seven years. The extended term for this class of felony is not less than seven nor more than 14 years.

Class 3 felonies include involuntary manslaughter, reckless homicide, and aggravated battery. The statutory term of imprisonment for an offender convicted of a Class 3 felony is not more than two nor more than five years. If aggravating factors are present, the extended term to which the offender may be sentenced ranges from five to ten years.

Class 4 felonies include crimes such as aggravated assault with a firearm, repeat domestic battery, and stalking. An offender convicted of a Class 4 felony may be sentenced to a term of imprisonment of one to three years; the extended term for this class of felonies is between three and six years.

If the offender has been convicted of the attempt to commit a felony, the sentence applied is that provided for the class that is one below the felony's actual classification. However, attempts to commit Class 3 or Class 4 felonies are punishable by the sentence prescribed for a Class A misdemeanor.

Misdemeanor Sentences

Class A misdemeanors are punishable by a determinate term of imprisonment of less than one year and/or by a fine of $2,500 or the amount that is specified in the statute defining the offense, whichever is greater. **Class B** misdemeanors are punishable by a term of imprisonment of not more than six months and/or by a fine of $1,500. Finally, **Class C** misdemeanors are punishable by a term of incarceration of not more than 30 days and/or by a fine of $1,500.

AGGRAVATING AND MITIGATING CIRCUMSTANCES

When determining the actual length of the sentence (between the minimum and maximum stipulated by statute, the court will consider both aggravating and mitigating circumstances. **Aggravating circumstances** are factors about the crime or the offender which increase the seriousness of the crime or make it worse than usual in some way while **mitigating circumstances** make a crime less serious in some way (see Schmalleger, p.372 and p.374). According to 730 ILCS 5/5-5-3.2(a), the factors which may be considered by the court as possible reasons for imposing a more severe sentence include:

(1) the defendant's conduct caused or threatened serious harm;
(2) the defendant received compensation for committing the offense;
(3) the defendant has a history of prior delinquency or criminal activity;
(4) the defendant, by the duties of his office or by his position, was obliged to prevent the particular offense committed or to bring the offenders committing it to justice;
(5) the defendant held public office at the time of the offense, and the offense related to the conduct of that office;
(6) the defendant utilized his professional reputation or position in the community to commit the offense, or to afford him an easier means of committing it;
(7) the sentence is necessary to deter others from committing the same crime;
(8) the defendant committed the offense against a person 60 years of age or older or such person's property;
(9) the defendant committed the offense against a person who is physically handicapped or such person's property;
(10) by reason of another individual's actual or perceived race, color, creed, religion, ancestry, gender, sexual orientation, physical or mental

disability, or national origin, the defendant committed the offense against (i) the person or property of that Individual; (ii) the person or property of a person who has an association with, is married to, or has a friendship with the other individual; or (iii) the person or property of a relative (by blood or marriage) of a person described in clause (i) or (ii). For the purposes of this Section, "sexual orientation" means heterosexuality, homosexuality, or bisexuality;

(11) the offense took place in a place of worship or on the grounds of a place of worship, immediately prior to, during or immediately following worship services...

(12) the defendant was convicted of a felony committed while he was released on bail or his own recognizance pending trial for a prior felony and was convicted of such prior felony, or the defendant was convicted of a felony committed while he was serving a period of probation, conditional discharge, or mandatory supervised release under subsection (d) of Section 5-8-1 for a prior felony;

(13) the defendant committed or attempted to commit a felony while he was wearing a bulletproof vest...

(14) the defendant held a position of trust or supervision such as, but not limited to, family member ..., teacher, scout leader, baby sitter, or day care worker, in relation to a victim under 18 years of age, and the defendant committed an offense in violation of Section 11-6, 11-11, 11-15.1, 11-19.1, 11-19.2, 11-20.1, 12-13, 12-14, 12-14.1, 12-15 or 12-16 of the Criminal Code of 1961 against that victim;

(15) the defendant committed an offense related to the activities of an organized gang...

(16) the defendant committed an offense in violation of one of the following Sections while in a school, regardless of the time of day or time of year; on any conveyance owned, leased, or contracted by a school to transport students to or from school or a school related activity; on the real property of a school; or on a public way within 1,000 feet of the real property comprising any school: Section 10-1, 10-2, 10-5, 11-15.1, 11-17.1, 11-18.1, 11-19.1, 11-19.2, 12-2, 12-4, 12-4.1, 12-4.2, 12-4.3, 12-6, 12-6.1, 12-13, 12-14, 12-14.1, 12-15, 12-16, 18-2, or 33A-2 of the Criminal Code of 1961;

(17) the defendant committed the offense by reason of any person's activity as a community policing volunteer or to prevent any person from engaging in activity as a community policing volunteer...

(18) the defendant committed the offense in a nursing home or on the real property comprising a nursing home...

In addition, according to 730 ILCS 5/5-8-3, the court may sentence an offender to a term of imprisonment which exceeds the statutory maximum (an extended term) if certain aggravating circumstances are found to be present. These are outlined in 730 ILCS 5/5-5-3.2(b):

(1) When a defendant is convicted of any felony, after having been previously convicted in Illinois or any other jurisdiction of the same or similar class felony or greater class felony, when such conviction has occurred within 10 years after the previous conviction, excluding

time spent in custody, and such charges are separately brought and tried and arise out of different series of acts; or

(2) When a defendant is convicted of any felony and the court finds that the offense was accompanied by exceptionally brutal or heinous behavior indicative of wanton cruelty; or

(3) When a defendant is convicted of voluntary manslaughter, second degree murder, involuntary manslaughter or reckless homicide in which the defendant has been convicted of causing the death of more than one individual; or

(4) When a defendant is convicted of any felony committed against:
   (i) a person under 12 years of age at the time of the offense or such person's property;
   (ii) a person 60 years of age or older at the time of the offense or such person's property; or
   (iii) a person physically handicapped at the time of the offense or such person's property; or

(5) In the case of a defendant convicted of aggravated criminal sexual assault or criminal sexual assault, when the court finds that aggravated criminal sexual assault or criminal sexual assault was also committed on the same victim by one or more other individuals, and the defendant voluntarily participated in the crime with the knowledge of the participation of the others in the crime, and the commission of the crime was part of a single course of conduct during which there was no substantial change in the nature of the criminal objective; or

(6) When a defendant is convicted of any felony and the offense involved any of the following types of specific misconduct committed as part of a ceremony, rite, initiation, observance, performance, practice or activity of any actual or ostensible religious, fraternal, or social group:
   (i) the brutalizing or torturing of humans or animals;
   (ii) the theft of human corpses;
   (iii) the kidnapping of humans;
   (iv) the desecration of any cemetery, religious, fraternal, business, governmental, educational, or other building or property; or
   (v) ritualized abuse of a child; or

(7) When a defendant is convicted of first degree murder, after having been previously convicted in Illinois of any offense listed under paragraph (c)(2) of Section 5-5-3, when such conviction has occurred within 10 years after the previous conviction, excluding time spent in custody, and such charges are separately brought and tried and arise out of different series of acts; or

(8) When a defendant is convicted of a felony other than conspiracy and the court finds that the felony was committed under an agreement with 2 or more other persons to commit that offense and the defendant, with respect to the other individuals, occupied a position of organizer, supervisor, financier, or any other position of management or leadership, and the court further finds that the felony committed was related to or in furtherance of the criminal activities of an organized

gang or was motivated by the defendant's leadership in an organized gang; or

(9) When a defendant is convicted of a felony violation of Section 24-1 of the Criminal Code of 1961 and the court finds that the defendant is a member of an organized gang.

In addition, the statute states that an extended term sentence may be imposed on an offender convicted of aggravated criminal sexual assault upon a victim under the age of 18.

The court may also take mitigating factors into consideration when determining whether or not to impose a sentence of incarceration, or when determining the length of such a sentence. The mitigating factors which may be considered by the court are listed in 730 ILCS 5/5-5-3.1:

(1) The defendant's criminal conduct neither caused nor threatened serious physical harm to another.
(2) The defendant did not contemplate that his criminal conduct would cause or threaten serious physical harm to another.
(3) The defendant acted under a strong provocation.
(4) There were substantial grounds tending to excuse or justify the defendant's criminal conduct, though failing to establish a defense.
(5) The defendant's criminal conduct was induced or facilitated by someone other than the defendant.
(6) The defendant has compensated or will compensate the victim of his criminal conduct for the damage or injury that he sustained.
(7) The defendant has no history of prior delinquency or criminal activity or has led a law-abiding life for a substantial period of time before the commission of the present crime.
(8) The defendant's criminal conduct was the result of circumstances unlikely to recur.
(9) The character and attitudes of the defendant indicate that he is unlikely to commit another crime.
(10) The defendant is particularly likely to comply with the terms of a period of probation.
(11) The imprisonment of the defendant would entail excessive hardship to his dependents.
(12) The imprisonment of the defendant would endanger his or her medical condition.
(13) The defendant was mentally retarded as defined in Section 5-1-13 of this Code.

RESTITUTION AND FINES

Several types of sentences that may be imposed require the offender to make some type of financial payment, either to the court or to the victim. A **fine** (see Schmalleger, pp.386-388) is a monetary payment made to the state. **Restitution** (see Schmalleger, p.369) involves repaying the victim for a loss sustained as a result of the crime. The death of the victim does not end the offender's requirement to pay restitution; if the victim dies before the payments are completed, all remaining payments must be made to the deceased's estate.

In some cases, the fine may be the only penalty imposed upon the offender by the court. However, it is also possible for the court to impose a financial penalty upon an offender in addition to another penalty. According to 730 ILCS 5/5-9-1(b):

> A fine may be imposed in addition to a sentence of conditional discharge, probation, periodic imprisonment, or imprisonment.

Illinois is attempting to increase the use of restitution. According to 730 ILS 5/5-5-6,

> In all convictions for offenses in violation of the Criminal Code of 1961 in which the person received any injury to their person or damage to their real or personal property as a result of the criminal act of the defendant, the court shall order restitution as provided in this Section. In all other cases, except cases in which restitution is required under this Section, the court must at the sentence hearing determine whether restitution is an appropriate sentence to be imposed on each defendant convicted of an offense. If the court determines that an order directing the offender to make restitution is appropriate, the offender may be sentenced to make restitution.

The amount of restitution to be paid is determined by the court and a time period in which it must be paid is specified. If a defendant does not pay the restitution within the specified time period, the court may order the sheriff to seize the defendant's real or personal property, and dispose of it by public sale, in order to satisfy the restitution order. The court may consider the defendant's ability to pay when making an order of restitution and may either require that restitution be paid in a single lump-sum payment or in installments. If restitution is paid over a period of time, that period generally is not more than five years, although this does not include periods during which the defendant is incarcerated. Payment of restitution does not mean that the victim is no longer entitled to sue the defendant.

OTHER POSSIBLE SENTENCES

Probation and Conditional Discharge

Probation (see Schmalleger, pp.411-413) is defined in 730 ILCS 5/5-1-18 as "a sentence or disposition of conditional and revocable release under the supervision of a probation officer." **Conditional discharge** is defined in 730 ILCS 5/5-1-4 as "a sentence or disposition of conditional and revocable release without probationary supervision but under such conditions as may be imposed by the court." The key difference between them is whether or not the offender will be under some form of supervision by a probation officer.

The topic of probation and conditional discharge is discussed in more detail in Chapter 8 of this supplement.

Periodic Imprisonment

A sentence of **periodic imprisonment** is defined in 730 ILCS 5/5-7-1(a) as:

> a sentence of imprisonment during which the committed person may be released for periods of time during the day or night or for periods of days, or both, or if convicted of a felony, other than first degree murder, a Class X or Class 1 felony, committed to any county, municipal, or regional correctional or detention institution or facility in this State for such periods of time as the court may direct.

The primary purpose of a sentence of periodic imprisonment is to allow the defendant to continue with certain community-based activities, which are listed in 730 ILCS 5/5-7-1(b) and include:

(1) seek employment;
(2) work;
(3) conduct a business or other self-employed occupation including housekeeping;
(4) attend to family needs;
(5) attend an educational institution, including vocational education;
(6) obtain medical or psychological treatment;
(7) perform work duties at a county, municipal, or regional correctional or detention institution or facility;
(8) continue to reside at home with or without supervision involving the use of an approved electronic monitoring device, subject to Article 8A of Chapter V; or
(9) for any other purpose determined by the court.

Periodic imprisonment generally may only be imposed on offenders who are at least 17 years of age. This sentence may not be imposed in conjunction with a sentence of imprisonment of more than 90 days.

VICTIM RIGHTS AND SERVICES

In Illinois, certain rights of victims are guaranteed in Article I, Section 8.1 of the Illinois Constitution. This section states that:

> Crime victims, as defined by law, shall have the following rights as provided by law:
> (1) The right to be treated with fairness and respect for their dignity and privacy throughout the criminal justice process.
> (2) The right to notification of court proceedings.
> (3) The right to communicate with the prosecution.
> (4) The right to make a statement to the court at sentencing.
> (5) The right to information about the conviction, sentence, imprisonment, and release of the accused.
> (6) The right to timely disposition of the case following the arrest of the accused.

(7) The right to be reasonably protected from the accused throughout the criminal justice process.
(8) The right to be present at the trial and all other court proceedings on the same basis as the accused unless the victim is to testify and the court determines that the victim's testimony would be materially affected if the victim hears other testimony at the trial.
(9) The right to have present at all court proceedings, subject to the rules of evidence, an advocate or other support person of the victim's choice.
(10) The right to restitution.

These rights are discussed in more detail in various sections of the Illinois Compiled Statutes. For example, 725 ILCS 120 is known as the "Rights of Crime Victims and Witnesses Act." 725 ILCS 120/4 restates the ten rights to which victims are constitutionally guaranteed. The Act also provides for procedures to implement these rights.

Victim Impact Statements

Schmalleger (see pp.382-386) discusses the **Victim Impact Statement**. Victim impact statements are written reports or verbal statements that are given to the sentencing judge and that describe the effects of the crime upon the victim. According to the Illinois Constitution and the ILCS, crime victims have the right to make a statement at court during the sentencing proceedings. 730 ILCS 5/5-4-1(a)(7) also states that, at the sentencing hearing, the court must:

> afford the victim of a violent crime or a violation of Section 11-501 of the Illinois Vehicle Code, or a similar provision of a local ordinance, committed by the defendant the opportunity to make a statement concerning the impact on the victim and to offer evidence in aggravation or mitigation; provided that the statement and evidence offered in aggravation or mitigation must first be prepared in writing in conjunction with the State's Attorney before it may be presented orally at the hearing. Any sworn testimony offered by the victim is subject to the defendant's right to cross-examine....

If the crime is one of reckless homicide, the victim's immediate family members (e.g., spouse, parents, guardian, etc.) must be given the opportunity to make oral statements at the sentencing hearing.

The Right to Restitution

During the sentencing hearing, the judge may consider imposing **restitution** to the victim as an element of the sentence, in addition to any other punishment that may be imposed (see Schmalleger, p.369). This generally involves requiring the offender to pay a sum of money to the victim as reimbursement for losses due to the crime. Restitution may also be in a nonmonetary form. For example, the offender may be ordered to replace the victim's property or may repair damages to the property rather than paying a sum of money to the victim. The issue of victim restitution is discussed in 730 ILS 5/5-5-6. Restitution may be ordered even if the judge sentences the offender to a fine or to a term of imprisonment in a jail or prison. In addition, victim restitution may be ordered as a condition of probation or conditional discharge.

The Right to Compensation

In addition to restitution, victims may be eligible for **compensation**. In 1973, Illinois passed the **Crime Victims Compensation Act** (740 ILCS 45). Through the resulting **Crime Victim Compensation Program**, victims of violent crimes can receive up to $27,000 of assistance for financial losses that were the result of a violent crime. Expenses that are covered by the program include medical expenses (including hospital costs, prosthetics, wheelchairs, eyeglasses, hearing aides, etc.), counseling expenses, loss of earnings, loss of services that would have been provided by a permanently disabled or fatally injured person, tuition reimbursement, and funeral and burial expenses (up to a maximum of $5,000). No compensation is provided for property damage or loss, or for pain and suffering.

The program only applies to victims of certain violent crimes. Victims of property crimes are not entitled to compensation through the Crime Victim Compensation Program. The crimes that are covered by the program include:

- first and second degree murder
- reckless homicide
- involuntary manslaughter
- kidnapping and aggravated kidnapping
- driving under the influence
- assault and aggravated assault
- battery, aggravated battery, and heinous battery
- criminal sexual assault, aggravated criminal sexual assault, and aggraved criminal sexual abuse
- arson and aggravated arson
- driving under the influence
- reckless conduct
- exploitation of a child
- sexual relations with families
- domestic violence

Only certain individuals are eligible to apply for compensation. Individuals who may apply for compensation in Illinois include:

- an individual injured in Illinois as a result of a violent crime
- a survivor of a victim of violent crime who is dependant upon the victim for support
- a parent whose child is the victim of a violent crime
- a child whose sibling is the victim of a violent crime
- a relative of a victim who incurred reasonable funeral expenses or medical expenses (or both)
- a child who witnessed a violent crime committed against a relative
- an Illinois resident who was the victim of a violent crime in a state or country that does not have a victim compensation fund

For a claim to be considered, the crime must have been reported to the proper authorities within 72 hours, the applicant must cooperate fully with the police or other law enforcement officers in the apprehension of the suspect, the applicant must not be the offender in the crime, or an accomplice of the offender, and the victim's injury or death may not have been substantially provoked or caused by the victim. The compensation claim must be filed within one year of the crime.

The Crime Victim Compensation Program is considered to be a last resort. This means that other remedies that are reasonably available, such as Medicare, health and life insurance, Social Security or Veterans benefits, and Workers Compensation must be attempted and exhausted before applying to the program.

CHAPTER 7

CAPITAL PUNISHMENT IN ILLINOIS

CAPITAL PUNISHMENT IN ILLINOIS TODAY

Schmalleger discusses **capital punishment** as a sentence on pp.388-400. The only capital offense in Illinois is the crime of first degree murder with at least one of eighteen aggravating circumstances. Because one of these circumstances involves murder committed during the commission of another felony, felony murder is a capital crime. The method of execution currently used in Illinois is **lethal injection**.

The minimum age to receive the death penalty in Illinois is 18; juveniles under the age of 18 may not be put to death although they may be sentenced to life imprisonment. For an individual to be sentenced to death, he/she must have been at least 18 years of age at the time of the crime, not the time of sentencing. Illinois does not forbid the execution of mentally retarded offenders.

As of April 1, 2000, there were a total of 167 inmates on death row in Illinois. Of these, approximately 63 percent (106) were black, 32 percent (53) white, and 5 percent fell into other racial categories. There were 163 males and 4 females on death row. The death penalty was struck down in Illinois in 1972, when the U.S. Supreme Court case of *Furman v. Georgia* challenged the constitutionality of capital punishment in the United States (see Schmalleger, pp.399-400). The Court ruled that the death penalty, as it was administered, constituted "cruel and unusual punishment" and therefore was a violation of the Eighth Amendment of the U.S. Constitution.

The death penalty was restored in Illinois in 1974 and the Illinois Supreme Court upheld the capital punishment statute in 1979 and 1981. However, there were no executions held in the state between 1974 and 1990. Between 1990 and June, 2000, there have been a total of twelve executions in Illinois. Five of those individuals executed were black and seven were white; all twelve were male. An additional thirteen individuals have been freed based on either innocence or lack of evidence.

It costs approximately $7,000 more per year to incarcerate an offender on death row than to incarcerate an offender in a standard state prison facility.

SENTENCING IN CAPITAL CRIMES

The only crime in Illinois for which the death penalty is a possible sentence is the crime of first degree murder. According to 720 ILCS 5/9-1, if a defendant is found guilty of first degree murder, a separate sentencing hearing is held to determine whether the sentence will be death or a lesser sentence. Before an individual may be sentenced to death, the following conditions must apply:

1. The defendant must have been at least 18 years of age at the time of the crime.

2. At least one of the 20 aggravating circumstances outlined in 720 ILCS 5/9-1(b) must be found to exist.

The statute lists a total of 20 aggravating circumstances which may be considered by the court and/or jury; at least one must be present for a sentence of death to be pronounced. According to 720 ILCS 5/9-1(f),

> The burden of proof of establishing the existence of any of the factors set forth in subsection (b) is on the State and shall not be satisfied unless established beyond a reasonable doubt.

The aggravating factors that may be considered during a sentencing hearing, and which are listed in 720 ILCS 5/9-1(b), include:

(1) the murdered individual was a peace officer or fireman killed in the course of performing his official duties, to prevent the performance of his official duties, or in retaliation for performing his official duties, and the defendant knew or should have known that the murdered individual was a peace officer or fireman; or

(2) the murdered individual was an employee of an institution or facility of the Department of Corrections, or any similar local correctional agency, killed in the course of performing his official duties, to prevent the performance of his official duties, or in retaliation for performing his official duties, or the murdered individual was an inmate at such institution or facility and was killed on the grounds thereof, or the murdered individual was otherwise present in such institution or facility with the knowledge and approval of the chief administrative officer thereof; or

(3) the defendant has been convicted of murdering two or more individuals under subsection (a) of this Section or under any law of the United States or of any state which is substantially similar to subsection (a) of this Section regardless of whether the deaths occurred as the result of the same act or of several related or unrelated acts so long as the deaths were the result of either an intent to kill more than one person or of separate acts which the defendant knew would cause death or create a strong probability of death or great bodily harm to the murdered individual or another; or

(4) the murdered individual was killed as a result of the hijacking of an airplane, train, ship, bus or other public conveyance; or

(5) the defendant committed the murder pursuant to a contract, agreement or understanding by which he was to receive money or anything of value in return for committing the murder or procured another to commit the murder for money or anything of value; or

(6) the murdered individual was killed in the course of another felony if:
    (a) the murdered individual:
        (i) was actually killed by the defendant, or
        (ii) received physical injuries personally inflicted by the defendant substantially contemporaneously with physical injuries caused by one or more persons for

whose conduct the defendant is legally accountable under Section 5-2 of this Code, and the physical injuries inflicted by either the defendant or the other person or persons for whose conduct he is legally accountable caused the death of the murdered individual; and

(b) in performing the acts which caused the death of the murdered individual or which resulted in physical injuries personally inflicted by the defendant on the murdered individual under the circumstances of subdivision (ii) of subparagraph (a) of paragraph (6) of subsection (b) of this Section, the defendant acted with the intent to kill the murdered individual or with the knowledge that his acts created a strong probability of death or great bodily harm to the murdered individual or another; and

(c) the other felony was one of the following: armed robbery, armed violence, robbery, predatory criminal sexual assault of a child, aggravated criminal sexual assault, aggravated kidnapping, aggravated vehicular hijacking, forcible detention, arson, aggravated arson, aggravated stalking, burglary, residential burglary, home invasion, calculated criminal drug conspiracy ... streetgang criminal drug conspiracy ..., or the attempt to commit any of the felonies listed in this subsection (c); or

(7) the murdered individual was under 12 years of age and the death resulted from exceptionally brutal or heinous behavior indicative of wanton cruelty; or

(8) the defendant committed the murder with intent to prevent the murdered individual from testifying in any criminal prosecution or giving material assistance to the State in any investigation or prosecution, either against the defendant or another; or the defendant committed the murder because the murdered individual was a witness in any prosecution or gave material assistance to the State in any investigation or prosecution, either against the defendant or another; or

(9) the defendant, while committing an offense punishable under Sections 401, 401.1, 401.2, 405, 405.2, 407 or 407.1 or subsection (b) of Section 404 of the Illinois Controlled Substances Act, or while engaged in a conspiracy or solicitation to commit such offense, intentionally killed an individual or counseled, commanded, induced, procured or caused the intentional killing of the murdered individual; or

(10) the defendant was incarcerated in an institution or facility of the Department of Corrections at the time of the murder, and while committing an offense punishable as a felony under Illinois law, or while engaged in a conspiracy or solicitation to commit such offense, intentionally killed an individual or counseled, commanded, induced, procured or caused the intentional killing of the murdered individual; or

(11) the murder was committed in a cold, calculated and premeditated manner pursuant to a preconceived plan, scheme or design to take a human life by unlawful means, and the conduct of the defendant created a

reasonable expectation that the death of a human being would result therefrom; or

(12) the murdered individual was an emergency medical technician - ambulance, emergency medical technician - intermediate, emergency medical technician - paramedic, ambulance driver, or other medical assistance or first aid personnel, employed by a municipality or other governmental unit, killed in the course of performing his official duties, to prevent the performance of his official duties, or in retaliation for performing his official duties, and the defendant knew or should have known that the murdered individual was an emergency medical technician - ambulance, emergency medical technician - intermediate, emergency medical technician - paramedic, ambulance driver, or other medical assistance or first aid personnel; or

(13) the defendant was a principal administrator, organizer, or leader of a calculated criminal drug conspiracy consisting of a hierarchical position of authority superior to that of all other members of the conspiracy, and the defendant counseled, commanded, induced, procured, or caused the intentional killing of the murdered person; or

(14) the murder was intentional and involved the infliction of torture. For the purpose of this Section torture means the infliction of or subjection to extreme physical pain, motivated by an intent to increase or prolong the pain, suffering or agony of the victim; or

(15) the murder was committed as a result of the intentional discharge of a firearm by the defendant from a motor vehicle and the victim was not present within the motor vehicle; or

(16) the murdered individual was 60 years of age or older and the death resulted from exceptionally brutal or heinous behavior indicative of wanton cruelty; or

(17) the murdered individual was a disabled person and the defendant knew or should have known that the murdered individual was disabled...; or

(18) the murder was committed by reason of any person's activity as a community policing volunteer or to prevent any person from engaging in activity as a community policing volunteer; or

(19) the murdered individual was subject to an order of protection and the murder was committed by a person against whom the same order of protection was issued under the Illinois Domestic Violence Act of 1986; or

(20) the murdered individual was known by the defendant to be a teacher or other person employed in any school and the teacher or other employee is upon the grounds of a school or grounds adjacent to a school, or is in any part of a building used for school purposes.

In addition, 720 ILCS 5/9-1(c) lists five mitigating circumstances which may also be considered by the jury and the court during the sentencing proceedings. These include but are not limited to:

(1) the defendant has no significant history of prior criminal activity;
(2) the murder was committed while the defendant was under the influence of extreme mental or emotional disturbance, although not such as to constitute a defense to prosecution;

(3) the murdered individual was a participant in the defendant's homicidal conduct or consented to the homicidal act;
(4) the defendant acted under the compulsion of threat or menace of the imminent infliction of death or great bodily harm;
(5) the defendant was not personally present during commission of the act or acts causing death.

According to 720 ILCS 5/9-1(d), a death penalty sentencing hearing may be held before the same jury that determined the defendant's guilt or before a new jury or, if the defendant waives his/her right to a jury, before the court alone. The decision as to whether the sentencing authority is the court or the jury is made by the defendant. The sentencing hearing proceeds under the same rules that govern the admissibility of evidence at a criminal trial and both the state and defense have the right to present evidence that pertains to the presence or absence of aggravating circumstances. They also have the right to present evidence relating to presence or absence of mitigating circumstances, but the rules regarding the admissibility of evidence do not apply.

If the hearing is held before a jury, the jury may not sentence the defendant to death unless they unanimously find that at least one of the aggravating factors exist. If they do not find that one or more aggravating factors exist, the defendant will be sentenced to a term of imprisonment. If the jury unanimously finds the presence of at least one aggravating factor, they must then determine whether there are any mitigating factors present that outweigh the aggravating circumstances. If the jury finds that the aggravating circumstances are not outweighed by the mitigating circumstances (if any), the offender will be sentenced to death. The judge is not allowed to overrule a jury's decision not to sentence an offender to death. However, if the jury decides on the death penalty, the judge does have the power to override this decision and sentence the defendant to life imprisonment instead.

If the hearing is held before the court, and no jury is present, the judge must determine whether or not any of the aggravating factors exist. If no aggravating factors exist, the court will sentence the defendant to a term of imprisonment. If the court finds the presence of aggravating factors that are not outweighed by mitigating circumstances, the court will sentence the defendant to death.

According to 730 ILCS 5/5-8-1(a)(1), for the crime of first degree murder, if the offender is not sentenced to death, he/she shall be sentenced to a term of imprisonment of not less than 20 years and not more than 60 years or, if any aggravating factors exist, to a term of life imprisonment.

Every capital case in Illinois is automatically reviewed by the Illinois Supreme Court. The Court does not have the discretion to reject appeals in capital cases. No defendant may be executed until his/her conviction and sentence have been reviewed by the Court. According to 720 ILCS 5/9-1(i):

> The conviction and sentence of death shall be subject to automatic review by the Supreme Court. Such review shall be in accordance with rules promulgated by the Supreme Court.

THE MORATORIUM ON EXECUTIONS IN ILLINOIS

On January 31, 2000, Illinois Governor George Ryan declared a moratorium on the execution of any Illinois death row inmates until a **Commission on Capital Punishment** has conducted a review of how capital punishment is administered in the state and has made recommendations to the governor.

The moratorium was prompted at least in part by the fact that between 1977 and 2000, more inmates on death row have been exonerated (thirteen) than executed (twelve), providing evidence of continuing problems in how the death penalty is administered in Illinois. Although Governor Ryan is a supporter of the death penalty, he has stated that he is concerned that, unless improvements are made in the Illinois justice system, an innocent person would be executed.

The Illinois Commission on Capital Punishment has a total of fourteen members. Governor Ryan has not given the Commission a timetable or placed any time limits on the Commission in the preparation of their report. The Commission is charged both with studying the problems with the state's criminal justice system and with specifically investigating what went wrong in the thirteen cases in which inmates were wrongly convicted.

Ryan has granted stays of all scheduled executions and, until the Commission completes its investigation, all lethal injections are indefinitely postponed. He is not pardoning these inmates, who remain under sentence of death, but has merely suspended the execution of their sentences. However, all condemned offenders remain on death row during this period. Illinois is the first state to totally halt all executions while it reviews its death penalty procedures. The Nebraska legislature passed a moratorium on executions in 1999 but it was vetoed by the state governor.

CHAPTER 8

CORRECTIONS IN ILLINOIS

THE ILLINOIS DEPARTMENT OF CORRECTIONS

The **Illinois Department of Corrections** is responsible for correctional facilities within the state of Illinois. The Department's statutory authority comes from the Unified Code of Corrections (730 ILCS) and the Juvenile Court Act (705 ILCS), although statutes such as the Criminal Code (720 ILCS) and Criminal Procedures (725 ILCS) also affect the Department's authority and functions.

Chapter 730 ILCS 5/3-2-2 outlines the powers and duties of the DOC. These include:

(a) To accept persons committed to it by the courts of this State for care, custody, treatment and rehabilitation.

(b) To develop and maintain reception and evaluation units for purposes of analyzing the custody and rehabilitation needs of persons committed to it and to assign such persons to institutions and programs under its control or transfer them to other appropriate agencies...

(c) To maintain and administer all State correctional institutions and facilities under its control and to establish new ones as needed. .. The Department shall designate those institutions which shall constitute the State Penitentiary System.

(d) To develop and maintain programs of control, rehabilitation and employment of committed persons within its institutions.

(e) To establish a system of supervision and guidance of committed persons in the community.

(f) To establish in cooperation with the Department of Transportation to supply a sufficient number of prisoners for use by the Department of Transportation to clean up the trash and garbage along State, county, township, or municipal highways as designated by the Department of Transportation...

(g) To maintain records of persons committed to it and to establish programs of research, statistics and planning.

(h) To investigate the grievances of any person committed to the Department, to inquire into any alleged misconduct by employees or committed persons, and to investigate the assets of committed persons to implement Section 3-7-6 of this Code...

(i) To appoint and remove the chief administrative officers, and administer programs of training and development of personnel of the Department. Personnel assigned by the Department to be responsible for the custody and control of committed persons or to investigate the alleged misconduct of committed persons or employees or alleged violations of a parolee's or releasee's conditions of parole shall be conservators of the peace for those purposes, and shall have the full power of peace officers outside of the facilities of the Department in the protection, arrest, retaking and reconfining of committed persons or where the exercise of such power is necessary to the investigation of such misconduct or violations.

(j) To cooperate with other departments and agencies and with local communities for the development of standards and programs for better correctional services in this State.

(k) To administer all moneys and properties of the Department.

(l) To report annually to the Governor on the committed persons, institutions and programs of the Department.

(m) To make all rules and regulations and exercise all powers and duties vested by law in the Department.

(n) To establish rules and regulations for administering a system of good conduct credits...

(o) To administer the distribution of funds from the State Treasury to reimburse counties where State penal institutions are located for the payment of assistant state's attorneys' salaries...

(p) To exchange information with the Department of Human Services and the Illinois Department of Public Aid for the purpose of verifying living arrangements and for other purposes directly connected with the administration of this Code and the Illinois Public Aid Code.

(q) To establish a diversion program.

(r) To enter into intergovernmental cooperation agreements under which persons in the custody of the Department may participate in a county impact incarceration program...

(s) To operate a super-maximum security institution, in order to manage and supervise inmates who are disruptive or dangerous and provide for the safety and security of the staff and the other inmates.

(t) To monitor any unprivileged conversation or any unprivileged communication, whether in person or by mail, telephone, or other means, between an inmate who, before commitment to the Department, was a member of an organized gang and any other person without the need to show cause or satisfy any other requirement of law before beginning the monitoring, except as constitutionally required...

(u) To establish a Women's and Children's Pre-release Community Supervision Program for the purpose of providing housing and services to eligible female inmates...

(v) To do all other acts necessary to carry out the provisions of this Chapter.

The Department has three operating divisions: Adult Institutions, Community Services, and Juvenile, and operates both adult and juvenile institutions. Additional divisions within the Department's Administration Section provide managerial and administrative support to the three operating divisions. The juvenile division of the Department, and the topic of juveniles in state institutions, will be discussed in the chapter on juveniles.

The Department's budget for fiscal year 2000 is approximately $1,122 million. The Department operates 27 adult prisons, 11 community correctional centers, and 7 juvenile institutions. Of these 44 institutions, 42 have been accredited by the American Correctional Association (ACA). The Vienna Correctional Center, a men's minimum security facility, was the first prison in the United

States to receive ACA accreditation in 1979 and the first to be re-accredited in 1982. The two facilities in Illinois which are not accredited are both recently-opened adult facilities that are currently in the process of seeking ACA accreditation. The Department also operates 10 work camps, 3 adult boot camps, and one juvenile boot camp. In addition, the Department is responsible for community supervision of adults and juveniles who have been released on parole.

PRISONS IN ILLINOIS

Schmalleger (pp.443-471) discusses the topic of **prisons** in detail, including the history and development of prison institutions. Illinois state prisons are run by the Illinois Department of Corrections. The Department's mission, as stated on their web site is:

> to protect the public from criminal offenders through a system of incarceration and supervision which securely segregates offenders from society, assures offenders of their constitutional rights and maintains programs to enhance the success of the offender's reentry into society.

According to 730 ILCS 5/3-6-1(b),

> The types, number and population of institutions and facilities shall be determined by the needs of committed persons for treatment and the public for protection. All institutions and programs shall conform to the minimum standards under this Chapter.

As of June 12, 2000, there were 42,898 adult inmates housed in the Illinois state prison system, including prison institutions, community correctional centers, work camps, and impact incarceration programs. Of these, approximately 65 percent were black, 25 percent white, and 10 percent Hispanic. The average age of inmates was 32 years. Only about six percent of the inmates are female, although since the 1970s the female population of the Department has been increasing at a faster rate than the male population. The majority of incarcerated offenders were committed by judges sitting in Chicago. Approximately two-thirds of these inmates were convicted of serious offenses, such as murder, rape, armed robbery, and large scale drug dealing. Over half of all inmates committed crimes against persons, approximately 25 percent were convicted of drug offenses, and about 20 percent committed property crimes (burglary, theft, fraud, etc.). There are over 1,000 inmates who are serving life sentences. The cost of incarcerating an adult offender is approximately $18,500 per year.

One of the biggest problems facing the Illinois Department of Corrections is that of overcrowding; as of February 2000, the Department reported that they were at approximately 160 percent of their planned capacity. Most inmates housed in adult institutions are double-celled or multi-celled. Schmalleger discusses the issue of prison overcrowding on pp. 458-461 and pp. 464-465.

Approximately 11 percent of offenders are housed in maximum security facilities, 35 percent in medium security institutions, and 52 percent in minimum security facilities. The Department maintains eight levels of security:

- Level 1 - Maximum Security
- Level 2 - Secure Medium Security
- Level 3 - High Medium Security
- Level 4 - Medium Security
- Level 5 - High Minimum Security
- Level 6 - Minimum Security
- Level 7 - Low Minimum Security
- Level 8 - Transitional Security

See Schmalleger (pp.466 and 469-470) for a discussion of prison security levels.

All Department facilities must provide certain minimum services to inmates. These are outlined in 730 ILCS 5/3-7-2, which states that:

(a) All institutions and facilities of the Department shall provide every committed person with access to toilet facilities, barber facilities, bathing facilities at least once each week, a library of legal materials and published materials including newspapers and magazines approved by the Director. A committed person may not receive any materials that the Director deems pornographic...

(c) All institutions and facilities of the Department shall provide facilities for every committed person to leave his cell for at least one hour each day unless the chief administrative officer determines that it would be harmful or dangerous to the security or safety of the institution or facility.

(d) All institutions and facilities of the Department shall provide every committed person with a wholesome and nutritional diet at regularly scheduled hours, drinking water, clothing adequate for the season, bedding, soap and towels and medical and dental care.

(e) All institutions and facilities of the Department shall permit every committed person to send and receive an unlimited number of uncensored letters, provided, however, that the Director may order that mail be inspected and read for reasons of the security, safety or morale of the institution or facility.

(f) All of the institutions and facilities of the Department shall permit every committed person to receive visitors, except in case of abuse of the visiting privilege or when the chief administrative officer determines that such visiting would be harmful or dangerous to the security, safety or morale of the institution or facility. The chief administrative officer shall have the right to restrict visitation to non-contact visits for reasons of safety, security, and order...

(g) All institutions and facilities of the Department shall permit religious ministrations and sacraments to be available to every committed person, but attendance at religious services shall not be required.

Thus, adult facilities provide a wide variety of services to inmates. **Residential Care** services include the basic requirements of humane living conditions, such as housing, clothing, food, laundry, commissary, and physical maintenance of the facility. **Security Services** include both internal custody and supervision and perimeter security. This is intended not only to prevent inmates from committing new crimes but also to prevent them from injuring other inmates. **Clinical Services** provided to inmates include inmate screening, security classification of inmates, individual and group counseling. Each facility also provides inmates with **Medical Services**, including emergency medical care, physical examination, and medical and dental treatment. The female offender population receives additional medical services tailored to their specific needs. In addition, inmates are provided with **Mental Health Services**. Approximately 10 percent of inmates housed in Department facilities are mentally ill, emotionally disturbed, or developmentally disabled. These individuals are provided with comprehensive mental health care, such as psychological and psychiatric testing, examinations, individual and group counseling, therapy, and specialized treatment programs. In addition, specialized mental health services for male inmates with severe mental illnesses are provided at Dixon Correctional Center while services for female inmates are provided at Dwight Correctional Center.

Each facility provides a wide variety of **Leisure Services** to inmates, ranging from sports activities such as soccer, softball, and running, to music, arts and crafts, and table games. Most facilities emphasize intramural activities as a way of involving large numbers of offenders. Facilities also provide **Religious Services**, including Bible study groups, prayer services, and Sunday services. Many special presentations such as Kwanzaa and Black History Month are also provided. Much of the religious programming is provided by regular volunteers.

Educational and Vocational Services are provided through the Department of Corrections School District 428, which offer programs through high school equivalency to adult and youth inmates confined by the Department. Programs include primary, secondary, vocational adult, special, and advanced education. One of the main goals of the program is to provide offenders with the skills and knowledge necessary to pass the GED. The Mandatory Education Provision of 1987 mandates that any inmate who is performing below the sixth-grade level in reading and math skills must receive a minimum of 90 days of Adult Basic Education instruction. In addition, District 428 contracts with various community colleges to provide advanced instruction, including college-level credit programs, in various institutions. There are a total of 50 different vocational programs available to inmates in the Department's Adult Division. **Special Education Services** are available for disabled adult inmates between the ages of 17 and 21 years of age. Most of the participants are behaviorally or emotionally disordered or learning disabled, although others are visually or hearing impaired or have a physical or health impairment of some type. Each facility offers some type of **Substance Abuse Services**. Participation in substance abuse treatment programs is voluntary. In addition, the Department provides **Sex Offender Treatment** programs to serve those inmates who have committed a sex-related offense.

Departmental **Work Programs** include the maintenance of work camps in which supervised inmates perform public service work in the community. Inmates housed in Community Correctional Centers or Work Release Centers may be employed, attending school, or involved in community public service work as well. Inmates is most adult institutions may also participate in the **Illinois Correctional Industries** program, producing goods and services which are sold to state and local government agencies.

In addition to secure adult facilities, the DOC also maintains **Community Correctional Centers** (CCCs). These are a form of pre-release center which allow inmates to transition gradually back into the community. CCCs provide inmates who are completing their sentence in the community with structured supervision; inmates live in the CCC and must participate in constructive activities (e.g., employment, vocational training, education, public skills work, etc.) for at least 35 hours per week. They may also receive alcohol and drug counseling while residing at a CCC. All CCC facilities fall into Level 8, or Transitional Security level. There are a total of 11 CCCs in the state. Five of these are located in Chicago, including two male facilities, two female facilities, and one mixed facilities. See Schmalleger (pp.456-457) for a discussion of the development of the community-based format of corrections and work release.

Whenever possible, CCC residents are placed in a facility in or near their home community. This allows them to more easily readjust to community life. Participants are allowed to visit the homes of relatives and friends for short periods of time, and receive more extended leaves as their release dates approach. Release time is a privilege that must be earned through strict obedience with the rules and requirements of the CCC program. CCC participants who do not conform to the program are returned to an adult institution.

PRISON LABOR

Schmalleger discusses the issue of prison labor and prison industries on pp.450-452. Illinois began the use of prison labor in 1867, when the first state-run prison, in Joliet, was opened. The prison warden contracted with firms in the local community to provide inmates to work in local factories. The prison also allowed businesses to set up privately-run factories inside the prison, using inmate labor to produce products. The income generated by inmate labor was put back into the running of the prison; the program was so successful that the prison was self-supporting within six years of opening. However, in 1904, the practice of using contract labor was abolished and replaced with the development of prison factories operated by the state. This new system gave each prison warden the responsibility for the farm or manufacturing operation in his own prison. Each prison industry program was run individually under the authority of the warden of that prison.

In 1931, a law was passed which prevented state prison industries from selling labor or products on the open market. This led to the passage of a state-use law which encouraged all state agencies and nonprofit organizations to purchase goods and services from prison industries rather than on the open market, when possible. In 1976, the prison industry program in Illinois was renamed the **Illinois Correctional Industries** (ICI) and the entire program was placed under central control, rather than under the diverse control of individual prison wardens.

Currently, ICI produces a variety of products which are both designed and manufactured by adult inmates in the state correctional system. ICI runs farms, factories, and service programs throughout the state, employing over 1,700 male and female adult inmates. Participation in ICI is voluntary and provides inmates with the opportunity to obtain useful skills, vocational training, and positive work habits which may assist them in employment situations after their release.

ICI is self-supporting and uses no state or federal tax income; all program monies come from the sale of inmate-produced services and products. Qualified customers of ICI include the state of Illinois, state agencies, local government agencies within the state of Illinois, public institutions, and non-profit corporations which are charted in Illinois. Purchases from ICI may be made without the need to obtain competitive bids from other manufacturers.

Products produced by ICI include bedding and linen (e.g., mattresses, pillows, sheets, towels, and gym bags), cleaning supplies (e.g., shampoo, hand soap, glass cleaner, and laundry detergent), a wide variety of clothing items (e.g., inmate attire, uniform shirts, men's shirts and slacks, women's clothing, gym shorts, pajamas, robes, undergarments, socks, belts, jackets, lab coats, caps, and gloves), floor care products (e.g., stripper, floor finish, mops, and dusters), brooms and brushes of various types (e.g., whisk brooms, street brooms, house brooms, toilet brushes, vegetable brushes), metal furniture (e.g., beds, foot and wardrobe lockers, storage boxes, and shelves), office furniture (e.g., desks, office chairs, bookcases), signage (e.g., street signs, barricades, and safety vests), nameplates and name tags, and various speciality items (e.g, cigarettes, mousepads, desk sets, t-shirts and sweatshirts, book binding, seals, and embroidery). ICI service operations include tire recycling, data entry services, eyeglasses and other optical services, furniture refinishing, microfilming, industrial laundry and dry cleaning, and telemarketing. Farms operated by ICI produce food items such as juice, milk, bread, and meat products.

In fiscal year 1999, the average number of inmates working in ICI per month was 1,482. In fiscal year 1998, ICI had $47.6 million in sales, producing a net profit of $3.7 million. Approximately 80 percent of the products manufactured by ICI are used within the Department of Corrections; the remainder are sold to agencies and organizations outside the Department.

JAILS IN ILLINOIS

In Illinois, the primary difference between a **jail** and a **prison** is that prisons are run by the Illinois State Department of Corrections while jails are managed by the county or local municipality. Inmates of state prison facilities are convicted offenders (usually of a felony offense) who have been sentenced to serve a sentence of incarceration of one year or more. Individuals residing in county jails may be convicted offenders serving sentences of less than one year or may be unconvicted suspects who are incarcerated while awaiting trial or sentencing. The average length of stay in a jail is much shorter than for a prison; some inmates may only stay a few hours while others may be held for several years while awaiting trial. See Schmalleger, pp.472-480 for a detailed discussion of jails.

According to 730 ILCS 125/1:

> There shall be kept and maintained in good and sufficient condition and repair, one or more jail facilities for the use of each county within this State. However, this requirement may be satisfied by a single jail facility jointly maintained and used by 2 or more counties. It shall be unlawful to build a jail within 200 feet of any building used exclusively for school purposes.

Currently, Illinois has 92 county jails. There are ten counties that do not operate a jail of their own. These counties house their sentenced offenders and pretrial detainees in a jail in another county, paying either a contracted rate or per-diem rate. The warden of each county jail is the county sheriff.

Jails in Illinois have three main functions:

- to house those defendants awaiting trial who were not granted pretrial release
- to punish convicted offenders who are sentenced to incarceration in a local facility
- to hold inmates awaiting transfer to other facilities

County jails provide a wide range of medical and mental health services as well as operating programs such as work release and boot camps. They also provide programs to address issues such as vocational and substance abuse needs and provide referrals to link inmates to local community programs upon release.

The Lake County Jail and Work Release Center

In 1989, the Lake County Sheriff's adult correctional division began operation. The division operates the **Lake County Jail**, which has housing for 602 detainees. In 1998, the jail had an average daily population of 543.

The Lake County Jail is a "new generation" or "direct supervision" jail (see Schmalleger, pp.475-477). The jail has eliminated traditional physical barriers such as bars. Residents live in "housing units" which have space for 24 to 60 inmates and are responsible for cleaning the entire jail facility. Each unit is directly supervised by correctional officers, known as "correctional technicians." Inmates who follow institution rules of behavior receive privileges such as access to day room activities, television, and recreation areas. The facility also has a maximum security area. Inmates are assigned to the direct supervision or maximum security units of the jail based on behavior, rather than on criminal offense. Inmates who are placed in the direct supervision housing units and fail to follow the rules are transferred to the maximum security area; to return to a general housing unit, the inmate must demonstrate positive behavior changes.

The facility provides detainees with a variety of programs oriented towards rehabilitation. These include parenting, anger control, and domestic violence classes as well as access to Alcoholics Anonymous, Narcotics Anonymous, and substance abuse treatment and education programs. The facility also provides various educational programs, such as adult basic education classes, GED classes, and English as a second language. Religious programs are provided through the work of seven volunteer chaplains and approximately 45 community volunteers who work in the jail each week.

Inmates in the jail also work on an inmate work detail, which has been in operation since 1997. The work detail includes six to ten sentenced detainees and two correctional technicians. Pre-trial detainees do not participate in the work detail. Each week the detail is sent out into the county to clear road debris from highways.

In addition to the jail, the Lake County sheriff is also responsible for the **Lake County Work Release Center**. This is a sentencing alternative for convicted offenders which allows them to maintain employment in the community while serving a court-imposed sentence (see Schmalleger, p.456). They also receive extensive counseling while in the program. In most cases, participants in the work release program are non-violent offenders. The Center, like the Adult Correctional Division, is run as a direct supervision facility. Residents are supervised in the facility by correctional officers; when they leave the facility they are supervised by field coordinators.

The Center has space to house 110 residents; during 1998, the Center's average daily population was the full 110 inmates. Participants are financially responsible for the cost of the program and must pay room and board fees to the Center. The Center is financially self-supporting. Approximately 92 percent of all participants complete the work release program with no violations.

COMMUNITY SUPERVISION PROGRAMS IN ILLINOIS

Schmalleger discusses the concept of community-based corrections programs in Chapter 11. In Illinois, offenders placed on **probation** are supervised by the county while offenders on **parole** are supervised by the state Department of Corrections.

Parole and Mandatory Supervised Release

Schmalleger discuses the general concept of **parole** on pp.414-417. On p.414, he defines parole as "the supervised early release of inmates from correctional confinement." Parole itself is not a sentence; it is a form of early release from a sentence of incarceration. Because Illinois has determinate sentencing, it does not have the traditional form of parole. Instead of traditional parole, Illinois has **mandatory supervised release** (MSR), which is an element of the statutorily-mandated penalties for felonies. However, offenders sentenced prior to 1977 may still be eligible for traditional parole. Individuals on MSR are known as parolees and are supervised by parole officers employed by the Illinois Department of Corrections.

After an offender has served his or her sentence of incarceration, he/she is placed under supervision for a period of one to three years; the length of the MSR term is determined by the level of seriousness of the felony of which the offender was convicted. Individuals convicted of a Class X felony must serve three years of MSR; those convicted of a Class 1 or Class 2 felony must serve two years of MSR; those convicted of a Class 3 or Class 4 felony serve one year of MSR. Misdemeanor offenders do not serve periods of MSR.

The state parole board is known as the **Illinois Prisoner Review Board** and is independent of the Department of Corrections. The Board was formerly known as the Illinois Parole and Pardon Board. It is composed of twelve members who are appointed by the governor with the advice and consent of the Senate. All members must have a minimum of five years experience in law enforcement, corrections, penology, sociology, law education, social work, medicine, psychology, another behavioral science, or some combination of these fields. At least six of the Board members must have at lest three years experience in juvenile matters and no more than six members may be members of the same political party.

According to 730 ILCS 5/3-3-2, the duties of the Board include (but are not limited to):

- hearing the cases of prisoners sentenced prior to the 1977 Act and who are eligible for parole

- determining the conditions of parole, setting the time of discharge from parole, imposing sanctions for violations of parole, and revoking parole
- determining the conditions of MSR, setting the time of discharge from MSR, imposing sanctions for violations of MSR, and revoking MSR
- hearing requests for pardons, reprieve, or commutations, and making confidential recommendations to the governor

Offenders placed on parole or mandatory supervised release are be required to comply with a variety of conditions. (see Schmalleger, p.415). The conditions to which all offenders on parole or MSR are subject are outlined in 730 ILCS 5/3-3-7(a), which requires that the offender:

(1) not violate any criminal statute of any jurisdiction during the parole or release term; and
(2) refrain from possessing a firearm or other dangerous weapon.

In addition, according to 730 ILCS 5/3-3-7(b), the Board may require other conditions of an individual parolee, including the requirements that he/she:

(1) work or pursue a course of study or vocational training;
(2) undergo medical or psychiatric treatment, or treatment for drug addiction or alcoholism;
(3) attend or reside in a facility established for the instruction or residence of persons on probation or parole;
(4) support his dependents;
(5) report to an agent of the Department of Corrections;
(6) permit the agent to visit him at his home or elsewhere to the extent necessary to discharge his duties;
(7) comply with the terms and conditions of an order of protection issued pursuant to the Illinois Domestic Violence Act of 1986, enacted by the 84th General Assembly.
(8) and, in addition, if a minor:
   (i) reside with his parents or in a foster home;
   (ii) attend school;
   (iii) attend a non-residential program for youth;
   (iv) contribute to his own support at home or in a foster home.

Offenders released on parole or MSR remain under the jurisdiction of the Community Service Division of the Department of Corrections, which is responsible for their supervision during their parole or release period and for providing various services to the offender. According to 730 ILCS 5/3-14-3,

> To assist parolees or releasees, the Department shall provide employment counseling and job placement services, and may in addition to other services provide the following:
> (1) assistance in residential placement;
> (2) family and individual counseling and treatment placement;
> (3) financial counseling;

(4) vocational and educational counseling and placement; and
(5) referral services to any other State or local agencies.

In addition, the Department assists inmates in custody in preparing for their release. One of the key responsibilities of the Department is to help inmates through the process of reintegration into the community. This is done through the use of a program known as the **PreStart Program**, which was introduced in 1991. PreStart is a form of "pre-release school" for offenders who are within thirty to sixty days of release, preparing inmates for their life outside of the prison. The program also includes a post-release component to provide assistance during the offender's transition from the prison to the community.

PreStart consists of two phases. Phase I is pre-release education and includes thirty hours of class work within the prison. Inmates learn a variety of basic life skills, such as how to fill out a job application, how to compose a resume, and how to get a driver's license. They also receive assistance with issues such as anger management and dealing with family and friends upon their return to the community, as well as information and assistance in accessing community resources such as substance abuse counseling. During the class, each inmate prepares an Individual Development Plan (IDP) which outlines specific personal goals and objectives as well as individual service needs. Phase II includes post-release assistance to offenders who have been released into the community. Inmates are supervised by parole agents who assist them in obtaining access to the various community services that may be available to them. Parole agents work out of PreStart Community Service Centers; currently there are 21 centers and three satellite facilities. As of June 30, 1999, there were 30,691 offenders in the PreStart Program being supervised by Department of Corrections parole agents.

In some cases, the Board may require an offender placed on parole or MSR to wear an **electronic monitoring** device (see Schmalleger, pp.427-428 for a discussion of house arrest and electronic monitoring). The Department of Corrections has been using **electronic detention** (ED) as a reintegration tool since 1989. It is also one way for the Department to deal with the constant problem of overcrowding in prisons. Inmates who are statutorily eligible and who are considered suitable for the program may be allowed to spend the last few months of their sentence on ED instead of in a correctional institution. The average time spent by an inmate on ED is 6.2 months. If an offender violates the terms of the ED program, he or she will be returned to prison to complete his or her sentence.

The program requires the offender to wear a transmitter strapped to his or her ankle; this sends an electronic signal to a monitoring device. Offenders are generally required to remain in their place of residence; effectively they are under "**house arrest**" or "house confinement." They are only allowed to leave their residence to go to work or school, to participate in court-mandated community service activities, or under other specific conditions which are approved by the probation officer. Participants are required to become involved in activities such as work, education, and substance abuse treatment programs and must submit to random urine tests.

Probation and Conditional Discharge

Schmalleger (see pp.411-413, pp.415-417, and pp.421-422) discusses the general issue of **probation**. In Illinois, probation is defined in 730 ILCS 5/5-1-18 as:

a sentence or disposition of conditional and revocable release under the supervision of a probation officer.

Illinois also allows for a sentence of **conditional discharge** which is defined in 730 ILCS 5/5-1-4 as:

a sentence or disposition of conditional and revocable release without probationary supervision but under such conditions as may be imposed by the court.

The key difference between the two sentences is whether or not the offender is supervised while in the community. Unlike parole or MSR, which are forms of early release from prison, probation and conditional discharge are themselves sentences. In Illinois, probation supervision is carried out at the county level, rather than at the state level.

The length of a term of probation or conditional discharge, as well as the conditions with which the offender must comply, are determined by the court. According to 730 ILCS 5/5-5-6-2(b),

Unless terminated sooner ... or extended ... the period of probation or conditional discharge shall be as follows:
    (1)   for a Class 1 or Class 2 felony, not to exceed 4 years;
    (2)   for a Class 3 or Class 4 felony, not to exceed 30 months;
    (3)   for a misdemeanor, not to exceed 2 years;
    (4)   for a petty offense, not to exceed 6 months.
Multiple terms of probation imposed at the same time shall run concurrently.

All offenders placed on probation or conditional discharge must comply with a number of conditions (see Schmalleger, pp.412-413) which are listed in 730 ILCS 5/5-6-3(a). These include:

- the offender may not violate any criminal statute
- the offender must report to any person or agency as directed by the court
- the offender must not possess a firearm or other dangerous weapon
- the offender must not leave the state without the court's consent
- the offender must allow a probation officer to visit him/her at his/her home or elsewhere
- if the offense of which the offender was convicted was gang-related, the offender must perform between 30 and 120 hours of community service
- the offender must (in certain situations) attend educational courses designed to prepare him/her for the GED or attend a court-approved vocational training program
- the offender must (in certain situations) undergo treatment at a court-approved substance abuse program

In addition, according to 730 ILCS 5/5-6-3(b), the court may require individual offenders to comply with additional conditions that may relate either to the nature of the offense or to the rehabilitation of the offender. These include:

- serving a term of periodic imprisonment
- paying a fine and costs
- work or attend an educational or vocational training program
- undergo medical, psychiatric, or psychological treatment or treatment for alcoholism or drug addiction
- attend or live in a facility for individuals on probation
- support his or her dependents
- make restitution to the victim
- perform reasonable public or community service
- serve a term of home confinement (which may include the requirement to wear an electronic monitoring device)
- comply with the terms of an order of protection issued by the court
- refrain from entering a designated geographic area (except under court-approved conditions)
- refrain from associating with or having any direct or indirect contact with certain specific individuals or types of persons
- refrain from using illegal drugs
- if a minor, reside with parents or in a foster home, attend school, attend a non-residential program for youth and/or contribute to his or her own support at home or in a foster home

The court decides which of these, if any, will be mandated for the offender.

Lake County Adult Probation Services

Probation supervision is carried out at the county level. In Lake County, the **Lake County Adult Probation Services** division of the county judicial system is responsible for the daily community supervision of all adults who have been sentenced to probation by the court. Adult Probation Officers carry out community surveillance of probationers and provide referrals to public and private agencies that may provide probationers with needed services.

The court may sentence certain felony offenders to a period of **intensive probation supervision** (IPS). Participation in IPS is for a minimum of twelve months; offenders who successfully complete the IPS program will be assigned to a probation officer who will provide standard supervision for the remainder of the probation sentence. Offenders in IPS meet frequently with Intensive Probation Officers (often many times per week) and must obey a curfew that is strictly enforced. The program focuses on maintaining regular employment, participation in public service work, avoiding the use of drugs, and developing a crime-free lifestyle.

The division also has several specialized units, including a **DUI Unit**, a **Domestic Violence Unit**, and a **Sex Offender Unit**. In addition, the division's **Presentence Investigation Unit** is responsible for preparing offender background reports for the court before sentences are imposed. Probation officers prepare between 500 and 600 presentence reports each year. The division's **Pretrial Services** program supervises arrested individuals who have been released on bond prior to trial. This program helps to reduce the jail overcrowding problem in the county and includes home visits and the enforcement of a strict curfew. Finally, the **Public Service Program** is an alternative sentence option that allows both adults and juveniles to perform community service for government, non-profit, and charitable agencies as a condition of their sentence.

BECOMING A CORRECTIONAL OFFICER

Schmalleger discusses the concept of the professionalization of correctional officers on pp.501-503 and discusses the job of probation and parole officers on pp.422-423. The **Illinois Law Enforcement Training and Standards Board** (ILETSB) sets and enforces minimum mandatory professional standards for both law enforcement officers and correctional officers in Illinois, setting training standards, ensuring that training facilities are adequate, and developing training and education programs (see Chapter 4 for a more detailed discussion of the ILETSB).

The minimum qualifications for employment as a correctional officer with the Illinois Department of Corrections are:

- be a resident of Illinois
- be at least 18 years of age
- have a valid driver's license
- have a high school diploma or GED certificate
- be a U.S. citizen or have a permanent resident card

The first training academy for correctional officers in Illinois opened in 1974. Classes are offered throughout the state. During fiscal year 1999, 7,962 employees attended training classes on a variety of topics. A total of 1,458 correctional trainees attended pre-service training. The Academy is quasi-military, with cadets and trainers wearing military-style uniforms.

CHAPTER 9

THE JUVENILE JUSTICE SYSTEM IN ILLINOIS

INTRODUCTION

Schmalleger discusses the concept of juvenile justice and juvenile crime in Chapter 14. Illinois is extremely important in the history of juvenile justice; the passage of the **Illinois Juvenile Court Act of 1899** created the first juvenile court that was separate and distinct from the adult courts in both purpose and procedure (see Schmalleger, pp.540-541). By the mid-1940s, every state in the country, as well as the federal government, had adopted legislation similar to this Act.

Today, the definition of **juvenile delinquent** in Illinois is similar to that used in the majority of states in the United States, as well as in the federal system. According to 720 ILCS 130/1a, the Neglected Children Offense Act,

> a delinquent child is any minor who prior to his 17th birthday has violated or attempted to violate, regardless of where the act occurred, any federal or State law or municipal ordinance.

The Juvenile Court Act (705 ILCS 1-3(10)) states that a **minor** is "a person under the age of 21 years subject to this Act."

The courts also recognize several special categories of juvenile offenders. A **habitual juvenile offender**, according to 705 ILCS 405/5-815, is defined as:

> Any minor having been twice adjudicated a delinquent minor for offenses which, had he been prosecuted as an adult, would have been felonies under the laws of this State, and who is thereafter adjudicated a delinquent minor for a third time shall be adjudged an Habitual Juvenile Offender where:
> 1. the third adjudication is for an offense occurring after adjudication on the second; and
> 2. the second adjudication was for an offense occurring after adjudication on the first; and
> 3. the third offense occurred after January 1, 1980; and
> 4. the third offense was based upon the commission of or attempted commission of the following offenses: first degree murder, second degree murder or involuntary manslaughter; criminal sexual assault or aggravated criminal sexual assault; aggravated or heinous battery involving permanent disability or disfigurement or great bodily harm to the victim; burglary of a home or other residence intended for use as a temporary or permanent dwelling place for human beings; home invasion; robbery or armed robbery; or aggravated arson.

In addition, 705 ILCS 405/5-820 defines a **violent juvenile offender** as:

> A minor having been previously adjudicated a delinquent minor for an offense which, had he or she been prosecuted as an adult, would have been a Class 2 or greater felony involving the use or threat of physical force or violence against an individual or a Class 2 or greater felony for which an element of the offense is possession or use of a firearm, and who is thereafter adjudicated a delinquent minor for a second time for any of those offenses shall be adjudicated a Violent Juvenile Offender if:
> (1) The second adjudication is for an offense occurring after adjudication on the first; and
> (2) The second offense occurred on or after January 1, 1995.

THE PROBLEM OF JUVENILE CRIME IN ILLINOIS

Juvenile crime is a serious problem in Illinois. Between 1993 and 1997, the juvenile prison population in the state increased by 80 percent; in several counties, the population of juveniles in prison doubled or even tripled. The percentage of juveniles incarcerated for serious crimes increased by approximately 14 percent during this same time period. In Chicago alone, judges hear an average of 1,700 juvenile delinquency cases each month.

In 1998, the violent index crime arrest rate for juveniles in Illinois was 910 arrests of juveniles (under the age of 18) for every 100,000 persons in the state ages 10 to 17. The arrest rate for property index crimes was 2,461 per 100,000, the arrest rate for drug abuse was 3,292, and the arrest rate for alcohol violations (including liquor law violations, drunkenness, and driving under the influence) was 193 per 100,000.

Between 1994 and 1998, the rate of delinquency petitions filed in Illinois increased by 26 percent (from 866 to 1,087 petitions per 100,000 juveniles). The delinquency petition-filing rate in Cook County (Chicago) was 54 percent higher than in the rest of the state.

In 1998, the rate of commitments to the Illinois Department of Correction's Juvenile Division was 89 commitments per 100,000 juveniles. As of February, 1999, over 80 percent of juveniles confined in state institutions were double-celled or multi-celled. The number of active juvenile probation cases in Illinois has increased by 33 percent between 1994 and 1998.

THE DEPARTMENT OF CORRECTIONS - JUVENILE JUSTICE DIVISION

According to 730 ILCS 5/3-2-5, the **Illinois Department of Corrections** is divided into two divisions: an Adult Division and a Juvenile Division. The **Juvenile Division** provides secure care and custody for juveniles committed to the Department by the courts, as well as rehabilitation and aftercare programs. The Division maintains seven youth facilities, or **Illinois Youth Centers** (IYCs). These are secure facilities, with security levels ranging from minimum to maximum security. IYCs house juveniles between the ages of 10 and 21. As of June, 2000, there were 2,116 juveniles in residence Overcrowding is a key problem in these facilities; the centers are currently rated to handle a total of 1,500 residents so the population is well over the rated capacity (see Schmalleger, p.572).

Two of the seven IYC facilities are **reception centers**. All juveniles are sent first to a reception center; male juveniles go to IYC-St. Charles while female juveniles go to IYC-Warrenville. Reception center staff obtain a wide variety of information about the juveniles, including medical and mental health information, educational levels, and behavioral histories. This information allows the division to determine the security level to which the juvenile should be assigned (to ensure the safety and security of the juvenile and of society) and to identify the specific programmatic and treatment needs of each juvenile.

Each IYC provides a group of basic services which fall into nine main categories. Basic **Residential Care Services** include food, shelter, clothing, administration, laundry, and the physical maintenance of the IYC. **Security Services** include both internal custody and supervision and perimeter security. This is intended not only to prevent the juveniles from committing new crimes but also to prevent them from injuring other youth in the facility. **Counseling/Case Management Services** are provided by trained counselors who work with juveniles individually and in groups. If the juvenile has substance abuse problems, drug/substance abuse counseling will be provided. The counselor also works with the juvenile on issues relating to his or her return to the community; the counselor will also work with the assigned parole officer to help ensure that the youth makes a successful transition from the IYC to the community.

The issue of **Secure Care** has arisen due to the increasing amount of violence committed by youth under the age of 13. In most cases, these juveniles are the responsibility of the **Illinois Department of Children and Family Services**. However, because of the need to focus on these aggressive young juveniles, the Secure Residential Youth Care Facility Licensing Act was passed (730 ILCS 175/45). This Act allows juveniles who are at least 10 years of age and who have been adjudicated guilty to be transferred to the custody of the Department of Corrections and to be placed in either a state juvenile facility or a state-licensed privately-operated secure care facility. Prior to the passage of this act, which took effect on January 1, 1995, juveniles could not be committed to the Juvenile Division until reaching 12 years of age.

Educational and Vocational Services are provided through the Department of Corrections School District 428, which is recognized by the State Board of Education. Each of the IYCs offers both elementary and secondary programs, with core curricula focusing on seven key areas: mathematics, science, health, social studies, communication skills, physical education, and vocational skills. In addition, special education services and literacy programs are provided, as are college-level courses (through contracts with various community colleges). Schools operate year-round. Each facility also provides youth with complete **Medical Services**, including emergency medical care, physical examination, and medical and dental treatment. Juvenile female offenders receive additional medical services tailored to their specific needs. In addition, juveniles are provided with **Mental Health Services**. Youth have access to psychiatrists, clinical psychologists, chaplains and religious services, and a variety of volunteers who consult on individual cases. **Leisure Services** are provided at each IYC by staff who are specially training in recreation. Programs include sports, arts and crafts, games, music, etc. Finally, the **Juvenile Field Services Unit** is responsible for juveniles who are on parole or who have been released from IYCs. This unit focuses on providing parole services, assisting with alternative community placements (if the juvenile is unable to return home after release), and placing youth in specialty programs such as substance abuse or sex offender programs.

JUVENILE FIELD SERVICES

The **Juvenile Field Services Unit** of the Illinois Department of Corrections is responsible for providing parole and aftercare services for juveniles released from IYCs. There are three district offices. The **Cook County District** handles all juveniles who were committed from or released to Cook County. The **Southern Parole District** includes juveniles from 63 counties and the **Northern Parole District** includes 38 counties. As of June, 2000, there were 1,610 juveniles on parole in Illinois.

Although the Unit's responsibilities towards a juvenile officially begins when he or she is released from an IYC, the development of a plan to reintegrate that youth into the community begins when he or she is assigned to the IYC. Each juvenile is assigned a parole officer long before his or her anticipated date of release, and that officer begins immediately to gather information about the youth. This information will assist the parole officer in determining the various types of support services that may be required or recommended as a condition of release, determine the type of community placement for each juvenile, and identify community facilities and resources that may be needed to meet the individual needs and requirements of each youth. Parole officers work not only with the juvenile and his or her family, but also with a variety of state agencies, such as the Department of Children and Family Services and the Department of Alcoholism and Substance Abuse.

Community placement becomes a key issue if the juvenile has been identified as needing some type of **alternative community placement**. Approximately 25 percent of juveniles in IYCs require alternative placement when they are released to the community. This may be because they require specialized care or treatment or because they cannot for some reason return home after release from custody. Types of alternative placement include foster homes, group care homes, residential sex offender or substance abuse treatment, or semi-independent living facilities. Pregnant juveniles may require placement in a residential facility that provides maternity services.

In addition, parole officers work to develop support services for juveniles. These may include individual counseling, family or group counseling, outpatient substance abuse or sex offender treatment and/or counseling, medical services, or advocacy services.

The average caseload of parole agents in the Unit is 52 juveniles on parole and 82 institutionalized juveniles (for which they are working with the IYCs to develop community reintegration plans).

WHAT HAPPENS TO A JUVENILE WHO IS ARRESTED IN ILLINOIS?

In Illinois, individuals who are under the age of 17 and who commit crimes are considered to be juvenile offenders. Most juvenile offenders are tried in the Circuit Court's Juvenile Justice Division. However, some juveniles may be transferred to the adult court. According to 705 ILCS 405/5-805, there are three main types of transfers. A **mandatory transfer**, which is discussed in 705 ILCS

405/5-805(1), involves the transfer to adult court of a juvenile who is at least 15 years of age, who is accused of a felony or forcible felony (e.g., murder, armed robbery with a firearm, aggravated criminal sexual assault), who has previously been adjudicated delinquent, and who committed the offense in the furtherance of gang activity. A **presumptive transfer**, which is discussed in 705 ILCS 405/5-805(2), involves the transfer to adult court of a juvenile at least 15 years of age who is accused of certain specified felonies (including most Class X felonies, aggravated discharge of a firearm, and various armed violence offenses). However, in these cases, the juvenile court judge has the option to retain the juvenile in juvenile court if he/she:

> makes a finding based on clear and convincing evidence that the minor would be amenable to the care, treatment, and training programs available through the facilities of the juvenile court... [705 ILCS 405/5-805(2)(b)]

Finally, a **discretionary transfer**, which is discussed in 705 ILCS 405/5-805(3), affects a juvenile who is at least 13 years of age. The juvenile court judge has the discretion to transfer the juvenile to adult court after considering factors such as:

(i) The seriousness of the alleged offense;
(ii) The minor's history of delinquency;
(iii) The age of the minor;
(iv) The culpability of the minor in committing the alleged offense;
(v) Whether the offense was committed in an aggressive or premeditated manner;
(vi) Whether the minor used or possessed a deadly weapon when committing the alleged offense;
(vii) The minor's history of services, including the minor's willingness to participate meaningfully in available services;
(viii) The adequacy of the punishment or services available in the juvenile justice system. [705 ILCS 405/5-805(3)(b)]

The first two factors are given the greatest amount of weight by the court.

The juvenile justice system in Illinois differs in several key ways from the adult criminal justice system (see Schmalleger, pp.562-563). Schmalleger (see p.562) provides a diagram of the general juvenile justice process. This is similar to the process used in Illinois. The Illinois juvenile court frequently operates less formally than the adult court, using non-adversarial proceedings. The terminology is different as well: the Illinois juvenile courts accept **petitions of delinquency** rather than criminal complaints concerning felonies or misdemeanors. In addition, juveniles are found to be **delinquent** rather than guilty, as in an adult court.

While under the jurisdiction of the juvenile court system, which begins at the time of **arrest** and continues until they are released from custody, juveniles are not allowed any contact with adult prisoners. After arrest, the juvenile will be taken to a **detention center**. Counties with no juvenile detention center send juvenile arrestees to a regional detention center they are not kept in adult jails. If a juvenile is placed in an adult jail facility, it will be for only a short period of time (e.g., several hours) and the juvenile will be kept totally separated from any adult inmates.

Within 40 hours of being taken into custody by the police (not including weekends and court holidays), a juvenile arrestee is brought before a judge for a **detention hearing** (see Schmalleger, pp.566-568). This is similar to the adult court preliminary hearing. At this time, the judge determines whether a crime was committed and if there is sufficient probable cause to hold the juvenile for trial. If the judge finds probable cause, he/she must decide whether to release the juvenile to a responsible adult (e.g., a parent or guardian) or to return the juvenile to secure detention while awaiting adjudication or other disposition of the case. In some cases, the juvenile may be diverted from trial and placed on court supervision for up to 24 months. Court supervision is carried out by the probation department.

Juveniles who have been charged with delinquent acts and who are awaiting trial may be required by the judge to comply with certain pre-trial conditions. According to 705 ILCS 405/5-505(1), these may include any of the following:

(a) not violate any criminal statute of any jurisdiction;
(b) make a report to and appear in person before any person or agency as directed by the court;
(c) refrain from possessing a firearm or other dangerous weapon, or an automobile;
(d) reside with his or her parents or in a foster home;
(e) attend school;
(f) attend a non-residential program for youth;
(g) comply with curfew requirements as designated by the court;
(h) refrain from entering into a designated geographic area except upon terms as the court finds appropriate...
(i) refrain from having any contact, directly or indirectly, with certain specified persons or particular types of persons, including but not limited to members of street gangs and drug users or dealers;
(j) comply with any other conditions as may be ordered by the court.

A juvenile must be represented by legal counsel when in court; 705 ILCS 405/5-505(1) states specifically that "no hearing may be held unless the minor is represented by counsel." If the child or his/her family do not hire private counsel, the court will appoint an individual known as a **guardian ad litem** to represent the child. In many cases, the guardian ad litem is an attorney; if this is not the case, the juvenile may get a public defender or private counsel to represent him/her. According to 705 ILS 405/5-610(1):

> The court may appoint a guardian ad litem for the minor whenever it finds that there may be a conflict of interest between the minor and his or her parent, guardian or legal custodian or that it is otherwise in the minor's interest to do so.

The fees are charged to the juvenile's parents or guardians, to the extent that they are able to pay. If the parents or legal guardians are unable to pay the fees of the guardian ad litem, they are paid by the county. The purpose of the guardian ad litem is to do what is in the juvenile's best interests. Prior to a finding of guilt, the guardian defends the juvenile. However, if the juvenile is found guilty, the guardian ad litem provides the court with a recommendation of the disposition that he/she feels is in the juvenile's best interest. This recommendation may include counseling, detention, or even incarceration. Thus, this task may place the guardian ad litem in the unique position of helping to incarcerate his or her own client.

A **juvenile court trial** differs somewhat from a trial in an adult court (see Schmalleger pp.568-569). Juvenile trials are not held in public, instead the courts are closed and only concerned parties and relatives are allowed in the courtroom during the case. Spectators are not allowed in and the proceedings are kept confidential. The press does not have an absolute right to attend juvenile hearings but individual judges may allow the press to observe. Juvenile court records, including the name of the juvenile, the charges, and the trial records, are sealed and may be seen only by individuals so authorized by the judge. To further protect the juvenile's privacy and ensure confidentially, juvenile trials are non-jury trials that are held before a judge only.

If the juvenile is found not guilty, he/she is released immediately from any detention, restrictions, or conditions placed upon him or her by the court. If the minor is adjudicated guilty, or if adjudication is withheld, he/she may be held in detention while awaiting disposition of the case at a **sentencing hearing** (see Schmalleger, pp.569-572). There are several possible dispositions. First, the juvenile may be sentenced to a term of incarceration. In this case, the juvenile will be housed in a juvenile facility run by the Department of Corrections; only juveniles are placed in juvenile prisons to protect them from contact with adult offenders (see Schmalleger, pp.570-572). Unlike adult sentences, juvenile prison sentences are generally indeterminate, although the juvenile may not be incarcerated in a juvenile facility for longer than the sentence that he or she would have received if he or she were an adult offender. In addition, the juvenile may not be incarcerated past his/her 21st birthday. Juveniles tried in adult court and sentenced to incarceration are usually placed in the juvenile division of the Department of Corrections until they become adults, at which time they will be transferred to an adult facility. Second, the juvenile may be placed on **probation** or **conditional discharge** (see Schmalleger, p.570). According to 705 ILCS 405/5-715(1),

> The period of probation or conditional discharge shall not exceed 5 years or until the minor has attained the age of 21 years, whichever is less, except as provided in this Section for a minor who is found to be guilty for an offense which is first degree murder, a Class X felony or a forcible felony. The juvenile court may terminate probation or conditional discharge and discharge the minor at any time if warranted by the conduct of the minor and the ends of justice; provided, however, that the period of probation for a minor who is found to be guilty for an offense which is first degree murder, a Class X felony, or a forcible felony shall be at least 5 years.

As with adult probation or conditional discharge, the court may require the juvenile to comply with certain conditions. Possible conditions of probation or conditional discharge are listed in 705 ILCS 405/5-715(2) and include requirements that the minor:

(a) not violate any criminal statute of any jurisdiction;
(b) make a report to and appear in person before any person or agency as directed by the court;
(c) work or pursue a course of study or vocational training;
(d) undergo medical or psychiatric treatment, rendered by a psychiatrist or psychological treatment rendered by a clinical psychologist or social work

services rendered by a clinical social worker, or treatment for drug addiction or alcoholism;
(e) attend or reside in a facility established for the instruction or residence of persons on probation;
(f) support his or her dependents, if any;
(g) refrain from possessing a firearm or other dangerous weapon, or an automobile;
(h) permit the probation officer to visit him or her at his or her home or elsewhere;
(i) reside with his or her parents or in a foster home;
(j) attend school;
(k) attend a non-residential program for youth;
(l) make restitution...
(m) contribute to his or her own support at home or in a foster home;
(n) perform some reasonable public or community service;
(o) participate with community corrections programs...
(p) pay costs;
(q) serve a term of home confinement...
(r) refrain from entering into a designated geographic area except upon terms as the court finds appropriate...
(s) refrain from having any contact, directly or indirectly, with certain specified persons or particular types of persons, including but not limited to members of street gangs and drug users or dealers;
(s-5) undergo a medical or other procedure to have a tattoo symbolizing allegiance to a street gang removed from his or her body;
(t) refrain from having in his or her body the presence of any illicit drug prohibited by the Cannabis Control Act or the Illinois Controlled Substances Act, unless prescribed by a physician, and shall submit samples of his or her blood or urine or both for tests to determine the presence of any illicit drug; or
(u) comply with other conditions as may be ordered by the court.

Regardless of the disposition, when the juvenile completes the sentence, he or she is released from the Department of Corrections.

TEEN COURTS

Several counties in Illinois have established **Teen Court** programs, which allow juvenile offenders to be sentenced by a jury of their peers, rather than in official juvenile court (see Schmalleger, p.568). Teen Courts are not trial courts; juveniles appearing in Teen Court admit their guilt and agree to accept the sentence passed by a jury of their peers. A juvenile court judge oversees the proceedings but the sentences are determined by teen members of the court. The program, which is essentially a diversion program for first-time misdemeanor offenders, provides juvenile offenders the opportunity to expunge the arrest from their record and to avoid the creation of a juvenile criminal record. The juveniles perform a variety of community service and other tasks ordered by the court.

The Knox County Teen Court

Knox County, Illinois implemented the Teen Court program in September 1995. The program is sponsored by the American Legion Auxiliary. Between then and April 1998, they processed a total of 282 cases. Juveniles sentenced in Teen Court provided over 7,000 hours of volunteered community service. A total of 29 teens were re-arrested after completing the Teen Court program and 27 were re-arrested prior to completing the program.

Of these first 282 cases, 176 defendants (62 percent) were male while 106 (38 percent) were female. A total of 250 (89 percent) were white, while 9 percent (26 defendants) were black and 2 percent 96 defendants) were Hispanic. The majority of the defendants (62 percent) were between the ages of 14 and 16, although the ages of participants ranged from 10 to 18 years of age.

Juveniles brought before Teen Court have committed a wide variety of offenses, including theft, burglary, criminal damage to property, illegal consumption of alcohol, disorderly conduct, battery, truancy, possession of marijuana and/or drug paraphernalia, and vandalism. Sentences issued by the Teen Court include serving on Teen Court jury, making a written and/or oral apology to the victim, attending workshops on decision-making, anger management, self-esteem, peer pressure, violence prevention, etc., making restitution, adhering to a curfew, participating in individual and/or family counseling, undergoing random drug testing, and visiting a juvenile detention facility.

Participation as a defendant in the Knox County Teen Court program is open to juveniles between the ages of 10 and 18 who plead guilty to misdemeanor offenses. Participation is voluntary and the juvenile's parents and/or guardians must be involved in the process. Either the juvenile defendant or the Teen Court coordinator has the right to terminate the relationship at any point in the process; if this happens, the juvenile returns to the referring agency. Defendants may only have one opportunity to participate in Teen Court; repeat offenders may not go through the program a second time. When a Teen Court defendant has successfully completed his or her sentence, there is no offense record. The court sends a request to the referring agency asking them to dismiss the charges originally filed against the juvenile. Juveniles who fail to complete their assigned sentence within sixty days are sent back to juvenile court for formal processing.

The Teen Court is run totally by teens; the only adult involved is the judge, who is generally a local judge or attorney who volunteers to participate. Teen volunteers serve as defense and prosecuting attorneys, bailiffs, court clerks, and jurors.

CHAPTER 10

DRUGS AND CRIME IN ILLINOIS

INTRODUCTION

Schmalleger devotes Chapter 15 to a discussion of the drug problem in the United States. **Drug abuse** is a serious problem in Illinois. The Illinois Department of Human Services estimates that among residents of Illlinois, almost 5,000 deaths per year are related to alcohol use alone. In Cook County alone there are over 16,000 drug offenders convicted each year; 70 percent of those individuals arrested for violent crimes test positive for drugs or alcohol.

The 1998 Illinois Household Survey on Alcohol, Tobacco and Other Drug Use, which surveyed over 8,000 adults (age 18 or above) in Illinois, found that the number of adults reporting current use (within the past month) of any illicit drugs increased from 2.1 percent in 1994 to 3.5 percent in 1998. The number reporting drug use within the past year also increased from 5.4 percent in 1994 to 7.6 percent in 1998. Similar increases were found for the use of marijuana. Current use of alcohol increased from 43.2 percent to 53.5 percent, although use of alcohol within the last year remained stable, with approximately 80 percent of those surveyed reporting having drunk alcohol at least once in the past year. Males were found to be much more likely than females to be substance abusers and to need substance abuse treatment.

The Illinois Office of Alcoholism and Substance Abuse estimates that at least 10,788 youth and 87,255 adults will require publicly-funded addiction treatment services each year. The need for treatment is much greater among males than among females.

On the bright side, drug use among juveniles in Illinois has shown some recent declines. The 1998 Illinois Youth Study on Substance Abuse, which surveyed almost 5,000 juveniles in grades 8, 10 and 12, found that the number of students reporting current use (within the last month) of alcohol, tobacco, or some other illegal substance decreased from 52.6 percent in 1997 to 49.5 percent in 1998. The number of students using alcohol dropped from 44.4 percent in 1997 to 40.7 percent in 1998; marijuana use dropped from 25.6 percent to 19.7 percent, and use of tobacco dropped from 33.2 percent to 28.4 percent. Cocaine use decreased from 3.3 percent to 1.5 percent, use of hallucinogens dropped from 6.0 percent to 2.6 percent and inhalant use dropped from 4.1 percent to 2.7 percent; use of inhalants is highest among younger juveniles.

THE OFFICE OF ALCOHOLISM AND SUBSTANCE ABUSE

The **Illinois Department of Human Services (DHS)** includes a number of state agencies. One of these is the **Office of Alcoholism and Substance Abuse (OASA)**, which is the state's primary agency for handling alcoholism and substance abuse-related issues. In 1999, Governor Ryan signed **Executive Order #9,** which appointed OASA the lead agency for all substance abuse services in the state and greatly strengthened not only the role of OASA but also the importance of substance abuse and addiction treatment and prevention in Illinois, making it a top priority in the state.

OASA is responsible for the development and maintenance of a statewide system for delivering treatment services to individuals who have substance abuse and dependency problems, as well as to their families. Many of these services are delivered in conjunction with the criminal justice system. OASA and DHS contract with community-based agencies throughout the state to provide treatment and rehabilitation to individuals in a community setting, thus allowed individuals to remain in or near their home communities.

Outpatient counseling and **intensive outpatient counseling** services include individual, group, and family counseling as well as methadone support, early intervention, and case management services. **Detoxification** programs are usually residential and provide support for individuals undergoing withdrawal from alcohol or drugs. **Residential rehabilitation** and **residential aftercare** programs offer rehabilitation services to individuals who need to remain in a monitored environment and require the support system provided by a residential facility.

The Illinois Department of Corrections provides substance abuse treatment to inmates housed in state institutions. The Sheridan Correctional Center's Gateway Foundation Program has space to provide treatment for substance abuse to 280 inmates. The three-phase program lasts for a total of nine months. Phase I, which lasts three to four weeks, consists of an orientation program. Phase II, which lasts three to five months, includes intensive treatment for substance abuse. Phase III lasts one to three months and provides the inmate with after-care services. The program has spread to other institutions throughout the states; fourteen adult facilities, two juvenile facilities, 11 work release centers, one recovery home, ten community drug intervention sites, and five boot camps offer substance abuse treatment services to state inmates.

OASA has developed a five-year plan to combat substance abuse in Illinois. Implemented in 1999, the plan has four main goals:

1. Conduct research to obtain information about publicly-funded prevention, treatment, and intervention programs in the state and about the need for services, possible gaps in services, service performance, and service outcomes.

2. Disseminate information as a way of increasing the awareness and involvement of researchers, policymakers, planners, funding sources, and members of the general public concerning research findings that are being implemented by publicly-funded prevention, treatment, and intervention programs in Illinois.

3. Develop special prevention, intervention, and treatment services for special populations, and improve access to these programs.

4. Use information and research to make informed planning decisions and improvements in the system, and to develop and maintain the most effective services to individuals who are either affected by or at risk of alcohol or drug abuse or dependence.

Each of the main goals has a number of objectives and action steps intended to ensure the goals are reached by the year 2003.

TREATMENT ALTERNATIVES FOR SAFE COMMUNITIES

Treatment Alternatives for Safe Communities (TASC) in Illinois is a non-profit agency that provides social services to individuals with health and social problems, including alcohol and substance abuse. The program provides substance abuse intervention services to adults and juveniles throughout the criminal justice system and serves as a link between the criminal justice system and the various community-based rehabilitative and treatment services available to substance abusing offenders.

TASC provides substance abuse assessment and recommendations for the Illinois court system, provides case management services, and monitors non-violent substance abusing offenders. The program works not only with inmates in the Illinois adult court and corrections systems, but also with post-release offenders and with juvenile offenders and youth who are considered to be at risk. In Fiscal Year 1999, TASC assessed 6,720 adult and 1,212 juvenile offenders.

According to 20 ILCS 301/40-5, an offender may be denied permission to participate in TASC programs if:

(1) the crime is a crime of violence;
(2) the crime is a violation of Section 401(a), 401(b), 401(c) where the person electing treatment has been previously convicted of a non-probationable felony or the violation is non-probationable, 401(d) where the violation is non-probationable, 401.1, 402(a), 405 or 407 of the Illinois Controlled Substances Act, or Section 4(d), 4(e), 4(f), 4(g), 5(d), 5(e), 5(f), 5(g), 5.1, 7 or 9 of the Cannabis Control Act;
(3) the person has a record of 2 or more convictions of a crime of violence;
(4) other criminal proceedings alleging commission of a felony are pending against the person;
(5) the person is on probation or parole and the appropriate parole or probation authority does not consent to that election;
(6) the person elected and was admitted to a designated program on 2 prior occasions within any consecutive 2-year period;
(7) the person has been convicted of residential burglary and has a record of one or more felony convictions;
(8) the crime is a violation of Section 11-501 of the Illinois Vehicle Code or a similar provision of a local ordinance; or
(9) the crime is a reckless homicide or a reckless homicide of an unborn child, as defined in Section 9-3 or 9-3.2 of the Criminal Code of 1961, in which the cause of death consists of the driving of a motor vehicle by a person under the influence of alcohol or any other drug or drugs at the time of the violation.

In addition, TASC programs have their own set of criteria to determine if an individual is acceptable. If any of the following apply, the offender will not be accepted into TASC service programs:

- the client shows no signs of physical and/or emotional substance dependence
- he/she has a significant criminal history of physical harm or the use of a weapon when committing crimes
- he/she has at least two prior probation or parole violations or at least two failed treatment or TASC episodes
- the nature of the crimes committed by the client shows no connection between the client's addiction and criminal activity
- he/she does not comply with TASC requirements
- he/she does not show any willingness to take action to remedy his/her addiction and criminal behavior situation.

To successfully complete TASC, all of the following criteria must be met:

- the client successfully and satisfactorily completed all the assigned treatment requirements
- he/she has remained substance free for at least the final four months of TASC
- he/she has found a stable living environment to go to when discharged from all TASC treatment requirements
- he/she has a stable and legitimate source of income (or will be a full-time student).

Violations of the TASC treatment contract may result in the client being unsuccessfully terminated from TASC and returned to the court for further processing. Major violations include:

- re-arrest for violent behavior
- re-arrest for manufacture or delivery of a controlled substance
- failure to maintain contact with TASC for over 30 days

Less serious violations result in written warnings; three written warnings or "jeopardies" will result in unsuccessful termination from TASC. These acts include:

- use of alcohol or drugs after admission into treatment
- refusal to undergo breathalyzer or urinalysis testing
- failure to comply with treatment rules and regulations
- failure to comply with the individual treatment plan conditions
- unexcused absenses from two consecutive counseling sessions or two scheduled TASC appointments
- hostile or uncooperative behavior towards TASC or treatment personnel
- re-arrest for a charge other than violent crime or the manufacture or delivery of a controlled substance.

In addition to adult services, TASC provides a variety of services to juveniles in Illinois. The TASC Juvenile Court services are geared toward delinquent juveniles who are also abusing alcohol or drugs. Many of these are specifically located in or around Chicago. The **Juvenile Court Drug Program** focuses on at-risk juveniles living in certain communities on the west side of Chicago (specifically Austin and Lawndale), who have been referred to the program because of drug or substance abuse charges. The **State's Attorney's Drug Abuse Program** refers first-time, low-level drug offenders in Cook County to TASC, who places these juveniles in community-based drug abuse education programs. TASC's **Evening Reporting Center**, diverts juveniles from the criminal justice system and provides an alternative method of supervision which allows juveniles to live at home and to attend school. The **On The Books** program, which uses a balanced restorative justice model (see Schmalleger, p.369 and 384) diverts delinquent youth who are involved in drug trafficking but who are not addicted to controlled substances away from the criminal justice system. Finally, the **Youth Enrichment Services Program**, which serves St. Clair County, provides life skills and vocational training for juveniles on probation. Program topics include self-esteem, substance abuse, job training skills, peer pressure, conflict resolution, and dealing with violence.

DRUG COURTS IN ILLINOIS

One new approach to breaking the cycle of drugs and crime is the concept of treatment-based drug courts (see Schmalleger, pp.611-612). This approach, which was first developed in Florida in the late 1980s, quickly spread to other states, including Illinois.

Peoria County Drug Court

Between 1988 and 1992, the number of drug violations in Peoria County increased by 384 percent; drug arrests increased from approximately 400 per year in 1990 to approximately 1,700 per year in 1995. Because of these statistics, the Peoria County Circuit applied for and received a federal grant in early 1998 to establish a county-wide **Drug Court**. This court provides treatment and rehabilitation services for non-violent adult offenders with substance abuse (drug and alcohol) problems. The court is operated in partnership with White Oaks Treatment Center in Peoria.

The decision as to whether an offender is eligible for the Drug Court program is made by the prosecutor; the determination is based primarily on whether violence was a factor in the offense committed. Participation in the program is voluntary. Eligible offenders are assessed by the White Oaks Treatment Center and a report on each offender is prepared for the court. This report is reviewed by the judge at arraignment. The judge then has the option of placing the offender on probation under the Drug Court program, with orders for specific treatment at White Oaks. First-time offenders who successfully complete the program will have the charges against them dismissed.

By the end of 1998, 112 offenders had been screened and processed through the Peoria County Drug Court. Of these individuals, 61 were accepted into the program and six had successfully graduated. Offenders placed on regular probation normally achieve a rate of negative testing for illegal substances of 73 percent; offenders in the drug court program had a 90 percent rate of negative testing for illegal substances during this period.

The Peoria County Drug Court program is currently being evaluated by the Center for Legal Studies at the University of Illinois at Springfield.

Cook County Rehabilitation Alternative Probation Program

The Circuit Court of Cook County received a federal grant in 1997 to develop programs for offenders with substance abuse problems. One of the programs developed for the Criminal Division is known as **Rehabilitation Alternative Probation** (RAP) and focuses on non-violent offenders who are on probation and who are subsequently charged with a Class 4 felony drug charge (possession of no more than one gram of a controlled substance); they are thus in violation of the conditions of their probation. The program uses treatment, intensive judicial supervision, mandatory drug testing, and a system of rewards and sanctions to break the cycle of crime and addiction among participants. RAP probation officers have caseloads of approximately 50 probationers; a significant reduction compared to other probation officers in the county.

To qualify for RAP, the defendant must be arrested for a drug possession felony while on probation, must have no history of violent crime, and must agree to be screened for the treatment program. Participation in RAP is voluntary; probationers who are accepted for the program will have the drug charge dismissed (although it is not erased from the offender's record) and will be sentenced to RAP on their probation violation. Completion of RAP is made a condition of probation and offenders who fail to complete the program will be prosecuted for the violation of probation.

There are a number of mandatory conditions that must be observed by all participants, including:

- participation in drug treatment programs
- increased frequency of reporting to the probation officer
- increased frequency of reporting to the court
- mandatory drug testing

The RAP supervision generally lasts 18 months. Offenders in RAP participate in individual and group counseling through community-based treatment facilities and are provided with assistance for educational needs, employment opportunities, vocational training and family counseling.

The court may impose a variety of sanctions if participants violation program rules, such as:

- reprimands from the judge
- increased frequency of drug testing
- increased frequency of reporting to the judge and/or probation officer
- writing assignments
- curfews or home confinement
- observation of drug treatment court from the jury box for one to four days
- confinement in court lock-up for a day
- confinement in jail

As participants complete successive phases of the program, they receive rewards that range from a handshake from the judge to positive words of encouragement from the drug court team to certificates of achievements. Participants who successfully complete the RAP program go through a graduation ceremony.

The first graduation ceremony was held in September 1999 and had 20 graduates; the March 2000 class had twice that many participants successfully completing the RAP program. A preliminary analysis of the first year of the program was conducted by Loyola University. Of the offenders who were accepted into RAP between April 1998 and June 1999, approximately 16 percent were removed from the program for noncompliance or for new arrests. The reviewers also found that rearrest rates were significantly lower for RAP offenders than for other probationers throughout the state.

APPENDIX

WEB SITES OF INTEREST

There is a wealth of information on Illinois and the Illinois criminal justice system available on the world wide web. Below are a selection of web sites that may be of interest to students.

GENERAL ILLINOIS WEB SITES:

http://www.state.il.us/default.htm
　　The state of Illinois web site. It includes links to various state agencies, the governor's web page, and is a great source of information about the state.

http://www.state.il.us/state/legis/
　　This is the official site of the Illinois State Legislature. It includes links to the web sites of both the Senate and the House of Representatives.

http://www.sos.state.il.us/home.html
　　The web page of the Illinois Secretary of State.

http://www.co.cook.il.us/
　　This is the home page for Cook County, IL.

LEGAL INFORMATION

http://www.legis.state.il.us/commission/lrb/conmain.htm
　　The Constitution of the State of Illinois is available online.

http://www.findlaw.com/11stategov/il/laws.html
　　This web site provides access to the Illinois Constitution and the Illinois Compiled Statutes as well as to other state codes.

http://www.ag.state.il.us/toc.htm
　　Another source for the Illinois Constitution and the Illinois Compiled Statutes. This site also provides access to the Illinois Supreme Court Rules as well as links to a variety of state and local agencies.

http://www.icjia.org/public/index.cfm
　　The web site of the Illinois Criminal Justice Information Agency. This site provides access to a wide variety of information on crime and criminal justice in Illinois.

POLICE-RELATED WEB SITES:

http://www.crisnet.com/locallaw/il.html
This is not an official government web site. However, it provides links to a wide variety of state, county, and local law enforcement agencies in Illinois.

http://www.state.il.us/isp/isphpagen.html
The web site of the Illinois State Police.

http://www.cityofchicago.org/CommunityPolicing/CPDhome.html
The web site for the Chicago Police Department.

http://www.co.lake.il.us/sheriff/
This is the web site for the Lake County Sheriff's Office.

http://www.sheriff.co.st-clair.il.us/
The web site for the St. Clair County Sheriff's Department.

http://www.cait.org/iletsb/
The web site for the Illinois Law Enforcement Training and Standards Bureau (ILETSB).

ILLINOIS COURT SYSTEM INFORMATION

http://www.prairienet.org/fordiroq/law/
This site provides access to recent court opinions.

http://www.ag.state.il.us/toc.htm
The web site for the Illinois Attorney General.

http://www.illinoisbar.org/
The home page for the Illinois State Bar Association.

http://www.IBABY.org/welcome.shtml
The home page for IBABY - the Illinois Board of Admissions to the Bar.

http://www.state.il.us/jib/default.htm
The home page for the State of Illinois Judicial Inquiry Board.

INFORMATION ON CORRECTIONS IN ILLINOIS

http://www.idoc.state.il.us/
The home page of the Illinois Department of Corrections.

http://www.state.il.us/defender/dpenalty.html
The web page of the Illinois Office of the State Appellate Defender, providing information on the death penalty in Illinois.

http://www.illinoisdeathpenalty.com/indexa.html
The web page of the Illinois Death Penalty Education Project. This is not an official government web site; it is sponsored by the Northwestern School of Law Center on Wrongful Convictions.

INFORMATION ON JUVENILE JUSTICE IN ILLINOIS

http://www.state.il.us/dcfs/
The home page of the Illinois Department of Children and Family Services

http://www.idoc.state.il.us/institutions/juvenile/field_svcs.html
Information on the Illinois Department of Corrections Juvenile Field Services Unit.

http://cyberfair.gsn.org/streaks/main/
The home page of the Knox County Teen Court.

INFORMATION ON DRUGS AND DRUG ABUSE IN ILLINOIS

http://www.state.il.us/agency/dhs/
The home page of the Illinois Department of Human Services.

http://www.tasc-il.org/Preview/index.html
The web page of TASC - Treatment Alternatives for Safe Communities.